Jackie After O

ALSO BY TINA CASSIDY

Birth: The Surprising History of How We Are Born

Jackie After O

One Remarkable Year When
Jacqueline Kennedy Onassis Defied
Expectations and Rediscovered Her Dreams

TINA CASSIDY

An Imprint of HarperCollins *Publishers*

*it*books

A hardcover edition of this book was published in 2012 by It Books, an imprint of HarperCollins Publishers.

JACKIE AFTER O. Copyright © 2012 by Tina Cassidy. All rights reserved. Printed in the United States of America. No part of this book may be used or reproduced in any manner whatsoever without written permission except in the case of brief quotations embodied in critical articles and reviews. For information address HarperCollins Publishers, 10 East 53rd Street, New York, NY 10022.

HarperCollins books may be purchased for educational, business, or sales promotional use. For information please write: Special Markets Department, HarperCollins Publishers, 10 East 53rd Street, New York, NY 10022.

First It Books paperback published 2013.

Designed by Jennifer Daddio / Bookmark Design & Media Inc.

Library of Congress Cataloging-in-Publication Data is available upon request.

ISBN 978-0-06-199434-0

13 14 15 16 17   OV/RRD   10 9 8 7 6 5 4 3 2 1

For my father

And my grandmother Genevieve Damaschi,
whose own third act still inspires

CONTENTS

Author's note: All dialogue and scene descriptions were drawn from firsthand interviews and/or archival materials, including photographs, newspaper accounts, and oral histories, among other sources. Citations have been placed at the end of the dialogue or scene.

Jackie After O

PROLOGUE

A merica. 1975. The Watergate trials ended, finding the defendants guilty and creating a generation of cynics. The United States was laboring to recover from a crippling oil crisis but had finally withdrawn from Vietnam. Tammy Wynette had a new hit song called "Stand By Your Man," while women still campaigned for the Equal Rights Amendment as they entered the workforce in record numbers and divorced in record numbers.[1]

It was a year when Americans were drained by politics, war, and a bad economy. Yet they were hopeful, as if they knew things could not get any worse. Two young men launched a company called Microsoft. From coast to coast, people flocked to discos to do the Hustle. In England, a band named the Sex

Pistols gave birth to punk and the British Conservative Party had chosen its first female leader, Margaret Thatcher, as Parliament passed the Sex Discrimination and Equal Pay Act.

Jacqueline Onassis was forty-five, living in New York, and going through her own confusing metamorphosis. The health of her much older husband, the millionaire Greek shipping magnate Aristotle Onassis, was rapidly declining, as was the diseased state of what was a second marriage for both of them. Her daughter, Caroline, was in her last year of high school. Jackie's younger child, John Jr., was a high school freshman, busy with his own friends and interests. Much of her day-to-day work as a parent was done, and aside from dabbling in charities and being the almost-estranged wife of a man who lived abroad, she had few other responsibilities outside of her very regular hair appointments, which happened to be once a week at Kenneth.

Like so many parents of grown children who find themselves suddenly single—or just unhappy at midlife—Jackie had begun to think more about herself and how, despite having such a full closet, she felt empty. She had enough money to continue living a life of leisure, albeit one where she was always trying to escape the haunting assassination of her first husband, President John F. Kennedy. But what ambitions and talents had she tucked away two decades earlier, to become—in succession—a wife, the First Lady, an international fashion icon, a grieving widow, a single parent, and later, a stepmother and jet-setter?

The world knew she was beautiful, stoic, and rich, with impeccable taste and a soft, little-girl voice that turned out marvelous French. It did not know, or perhaps did not care, that she was interested in history and architecture, that she was a talented writer, a voracious reader, and a person of ambitions of her own. Now, on the precipice of 1975, when society all around her was changing, Jackie was beginning to wonder how she should spend the rest of her life. What would make her truly happy? These were especially difficult questions for a woman whose pre–World War II generation and social stratum had bred her for nothing more than marriage and motherhood and the attendant accessory decorating and volunteering opportunities.

The simple title she had earned—truly earned—twice, was wife. Now, she was about to become something else.

CHAPTER ONE

The Wife

In 1953, Jack Kennedy was a freshman senator from Massachusetts with a bothersome back and enormous aspirations. He had just married a young woman named Jacqueline Bouvier, whom he had met at the home of mutual friends in Washington, DC, the city where Jackie, with wavy, short brown hair, had been working as a newspaper photographer, taking headshots for a brief question-and-answer column she wrote about her subjects.

Jack wasn't the only Kennedy busy in the capital. His younger brother Robert was assistant counsel to Roy Cohn, the chief investigator working for Senator Joseph McCarthy's anti-Communist crusade. Bobby had begun digging through records in an attempt to uncover those who might have been trading with Communist China, and he suspected a mysterious Greek, Aristotle Onassis, was among them. Bobby could not find proof of any red links, but he instead found that using a front corporation in America five years earlier Onassis had illegally bought ten US surplus tankers that were forbidden for purchase by foreigners. Bobby had a win; soon a federal grand jury handed down an indictment of Onassis, who was ordered to pay a $7 million fine.

"This Irish fuck wants to bury me," Onassis complained to a friend.[1]

But instead of avoiding the Kennedys, Onassis pulled them into his orbit.

A few years after the indictment, Jack and his bride were on vacation in Cannes visiting Jack's father—Joseph P. Kennedy, the former ambassador to the United Kingdom—and doing what fine young things did in the Riviera then: they basked on the beach and went out to dinner with the head of Fiat, Gianni Agnelli, and his wife, Marella. But one of the nights was even more special. Winston Churchill was aboard Onassis's ship, anchored off Monaco, where the Greek also based his family and business. Churchill sprung the idea to invite the Kennedys, to see if JFK was indeed presidential material, as he had been hearing.

Jack was eager to meet Churchill, a hero of his since the war. He had devoured the former prime minister's books, even giving a nod to a 1938 Churchill title, *While England Slept*, when he published his Harvard thesis, *Why England Slept*, two years later. But Churchill, by the time Jack met him, was a round and confused octogenarian who had no idea which guest Jack was when he arrived for cocktails aboard the lavish *Christina* with Jackie and the Agnellis.

"I knew your father so well," Churchill said, leaning in to the wrong person on the boat. Jackie realized that the old man was "gaga" and felt sorry her husband was meeting him "too late."[2] While Jack struggled to make conversation with the old man, Onassis absorbed Jackie with his eyes, noting her expensive but simple white suit as he gave her a tour of his 315-foot yacht. The ship was a former Canadian frigate on which he had spent more than $4 million to install forty-two extension telephones, a surgical operating room, Siena marble baths, a mosaic dance floor that could open to a pool, and bar stools covered in whale scrotum.[3] (He used to ask women if they enjoyed "sitting on the largest balls in the world."[4])

But the aesthetic matched Onassis's swaggering personality. With his smooth olive skin, habitual Cuban cigar, dousing of cologne, and hair thick with Brilliantine, he could be magnetic. He had a capacity to listen, observe, and collect beautiful women. But his charms did not appear to work on Jackie that night. He noticed that she was pleasant but aloof during the tour, making mindless small talk with him "in her little voice."

"I must ask you to leave by 7:30," Onassis told the group. "Sir Winston dines sharp at 8:15."[5]

After the group left, Costa Gratsos, a close friend of Onassis, guessed what was on his boss's mind.

"Don't fuck up her life just to get even with Bobby," Gratsos said.[6]

Jackie's next fateful meeting with Onassis came during the presidency after her infant son Patrick, born prematurely, died when he was just two days old in August 1963. The Kennedys were devastated, and Jackie, on Cape Cod, summoned the strength to call her younger sister, Lee Radziwill, to tell her the horrible news. Although Lee was married for the second time to Stanislas "Stas" Radziwill, a Polish prince, and they were living in London with their two young children, Anthony and Tina, Lee had developed a relationship with Onassis in the intervening years and was with him in Greece when the First Lady phoned her.

Invite her over for a rest, Onassis suggested to Lee.

Jackie left for her two-week trip to Greece in October, and, still weak from her wrenching cesarean, needed oxygen on the flight over. The president, facing a tough reelection campaign, stayed behind with his mother, Rose, by his side to greet foreign dignitaries at the White House.[7]

The media seized on the question of why Jackie would sail with a man who had been indicted and fined by the US government. Indeed, his FBI file was as thick as two telephone books, full of memos about potential un-American activities during World War II and, later, Cuba.[8]

They also wanted to know why Franklin D. Roosevelt Jr.,

then undersecretary of commerce who was serving as a kind of old-fashioned chaperone on the trip, would stay on a yacht owned by a man whose nautical empire the US government partly regulated.[9] And it was no ordinary boat.

Floating in the Mediterranean, the *Christina's* passengers—indulged with fresh figs and strawberries, caviar, ten extra servants, two hairdressers, and a band—were initially unaware that Jackie's recuperative cruise had turned into a scandal in America. They passed the days floating between Istanbul, Marrakesh, and islands in the Aegean, with Onassis impressing Jackie with his knowledge about art and history, bringing alive the ruins in Crete and those at the Oracle at Delphi, where, when she stumbled in a hole, he was there to help her up. Between the sightseeing and Onassis's history lessons in highly remote locations, she, in turn, confided in him about her life lived in public with an imperfect spouse. He listened intently, tried to be supportive. He also encouraged her to stick by her husband's side and campaign with him that fall. She took his advice.[10]

A month later, on November 22, 1963, Dallas was her first official reelection campaign trip. And, sadly, it was also her last, as bullets shattered the president's windpipe and skull, sending a chunk of his brain in an arc through the air, spilling his blood into the lap of Jackie's pink Chanel skirt in an open-top limousine.

Onassis was one of the few outsiders to visit Jackie at the White House on the day of Kennedy's funeral.[11] And they slowly became closer. He brought gifts to her kids and visited them on

Cape Cod, where they playfully buried him in the sand. He could still charm an aging Churchill as well as a string of remarkable women, from his first wife, Tina—the daughter of an even richer Greek tanker tycoon—to his longtime mistress, the opera soprano Maria Callas, and, eventually, Jacqueline Kennedy. He was a buccaneer of a businessman, able to pull off such complex deals that his tanker *Tina Onassis* "was built in Germany, mortgaged in the United States, insured in London, financially controlled from Monaco and manned by Greeks. It flew the flag of Liberia." [12]

Onassis fit a pattern for Jackie, who had relied on a series of men with means and strong personalities throughout her life. First, there was her father, "Black Jack," the stockbroker who lost more money than he made, who drank and cheated but still indulged his daughters Jackie and Lee after their mother divorced him; her stepfather, Hugh D. Auchincloss, whose inherited Standard Oil wealth enabled the family to live among high society, even though they eventually ran low on cash; JFK, whose family money was built on stocks, the movie business, real estate, and a touch of bootlegging; and then Bobby Kennedy, whose fighting spirit and near-constant presence—to the annoyance of his wife, Ethel—protected Jackie in her darkest days.

For several years after the assassination, Jackie struggled to bring equilibrium back to her life, moving to New York, making her children feel secure, establishing new routines, and settling back into Manhattan society. It was not until after

Robert Kennedy's murder in June 1968 that a devastated and terrified Jackie thought she and her children were also homicide targets and, shaken to her core, was prepared to turn her back on America. Not surprisingly, Onassis was there to rescue her in her grief with his boat—and give her shelter on his own private island, Skorpios.

Skorpios, in the Ionian Sea between the west coast of Greece and the heel of Italy, was aptly named for being shaped like a scorpion, with land like a curled tail at one end and two pincers at the other. It was a place of unsurpassed freedom and luxury, a place Onassis, one of the richest men in the world, had bought for about $100,000 a dozen years earlier in 1963.[13] He then spent another $10 million to domesticate its rugged beauty, to raise farm animals, and to plant vineyards, fig trees, olive groves, and flowers. It was a place where the scent of eucalyptus and jasmine mixed with briny air, where bathing suits seemed superfluous, and waiters in white gloves served beluga caviar and Dom Pérignon.

It was there, on October 20, 1968, that Jacqueline Kennedy stunned so many by marrying Onassis. With a prenuptial agreement in place that had been negotiated by her former brother-in-law US senator Edward M. (Ted) Kennedy and her financial adviser, André Meyer, the contract made it clear that the $200,000 in yearly support from the Kennedys and the $10,000 annual widow's pension from the US government would cease as a result of the wedding. Onassis agreed to give her spending money and $3 million up front, as well as annual interest on million-dollar trusts for John and Caroline. Although tabloids later widely reported that the prenuptial agreement had 170 clauses covering every detail of how their life together should be—including their frequency of sex—the author of that claim later admitted to inventing those details.[14]

Clearly, money was not an issue—in the beginning. But it did become one of several obstacles in their marriage. Onassis was the opposite of her first husband in appearance, age, and approach to many aspects of life. He was mercurial, could be crude, and was old-fashioned about many things, especially his treatment of women. He flaunted his affair with Maria Callas, before and after he married Jackie, and was even photographed in May 1970 with her at Maxim's in Paris.[15]

Indeed, Onassis was an incongruous mate for America's queen: twenty-nine years older than Jackie, he was more than two inches shorter at just five foot five, and heavier and rougher than the horsy-artsy-intellectual crowd with which she was embedded. He was a divorcee and a world-class womanizer. She was the good Catholic who had learned to turn the other cheek in her first marriage. He loved bouzouki music and smashed pottery in Greek tavernas, one night running up a bill as high as $1,000 for all the dishware he threw.[16] She loved the theater. He didn't. He was a night person, typically waking when she was eating lunch. Onassis often wore a dark suit and tie, even in the summer. Jackie, by contrast, was always impeccably dressed

October 20, 1968. Jackie, wearing Valentino, and Aristotle Onassis, at their wedding on his private island, Skorpios. *(Bettman/CORBIS)*

according to season and occasion, and a regular at Valentino—who had made the ivory skirt and lace sweater [17] she wore for their Greek wedding.

Whatever reasons she may have had for marrying Onassis—love, money, security—even her admirers were perplexed by her choice.

When her friend Truman Capote asked her why, she said, "I can't very well marry a dentist from New Jersey!" [18]

Other friends told her she was going to fall off her pedestal if she married Onassis.

"That's better than freezing there," she scoffed. [19]

Caroline and John "would have been happy to stay around

the penny candy store in Hyannis" rather than go to Greece, but it wasn't up to them.[20]

Onassis had lived a large life. Born in Turkey to an overbearing father and a mother who died when he was twelve, his formative years were tumultuous and oppressive. Although his father remarried, producing two more of his three sisters, the family was forced into exile in Athens during the political upheaval caused by Atatürk, the revolutionary who transformed Turkey from a caliphate to a republic. But Onassis did not stay in Athens for long, leaving for Argentina to seek his fortune with as little as $60 in his pocket.

In Buenos Aires, he bunked in a cheap boardinghouse above a dance hall (which instilled his lifelong love of tango) and worked as a telephone operator, where he polished his international language and business skills through eavesdropping on calls. Eventually, he bought tobacco from Greek sailors, and peddled it on a cart. By 1930, as smoking became ever more popular, Onassis had built the tobacco business into a million-dollar company, motivating him to expand his enterprises. He bought an abandoned wooden ship, frozen in ice in Nova Scotia, sight unseen for $35,000 during the Great Depression. The ship would be his first of many.[21]

At his peak, the man nicknamed the "Golden Greek" was controlling some one hundred companies in a dozen countries, including hotels, banks, piers, real estate, and an enormous fleet of seafaring vessels, separate from his yacht, which cost $500,000 a year to run.[22] Onassis, never one to sit still for long, had moved from Monaco to Skorpios as his home base, where he had a helipad, airstrip, marina, and the *Christina*, on which he preferred to sleep and spend his time.[23]

For a handful of summers and school vacations, the 350-acre cypress-covered island was a safe retreat for Jackie, her children, sister, and New York–society friends. There, they could lounge on the yacht or at his stucco, hill-perched villa, which had been white until he painted it pink for his wife, as if trying to erase memories of another exotic white house she had lived in. Jackie relished her time on the island, meticulously decorating the villa with Greek antiques, books, and flokati rugs to soften the terra-cotta floors. When she was not shopping in Athens or reading on the beach, she had a six-horse barn to visit and miles of riding paths that were hers alone.

But paradise was a fiction, a place where Onassis had dynamited rock to build roads, ravaged trees from other islands, laid imported grass from South Africa, and sprayed chemicals to kill snakes and insects.[24] This island was indeed a place that stung on many levels, its natural beauty in jarring juxtaposition to the physical, emotional, and financial devastation unfolding there.

Onassis lost his only son, Alexander, in what the father believed to be a suspicious plane crash in January 1973. Within a year,

Onassis was offering a $500,000 reward for anyone with information about whether the Piaggio plane Alex was flying in was tampered with—or suffered from improper maintenance, or pilot's error—but the cause was never determined.[25] His body was laid to rest next to the chapel where his father's wedding to Jackie had taken place. Onassis would visit the grave often, and his son's death plunged the old man into an isolating depression that made him mean, paranoid, and an even more difficult husband.

After five years of marriage, during which he basked in Jackie's light, Onassis was also shadowed by the legacy of JFK, whose tenth assassination anniversary—and its many official events—was coming up that year. Add to that the discord that two sets of stepchildren can create, arguments over money—specifically Jackie's spending on clothes and shoes—Callas, and the differences that resulted from their respective cultures, ages, geographies, and interests, and the relationship was, not surprisingly, wearing thin. And after Alex's death, Onassis's inner turmoil made him angry, withdrawn, and preoccupied.

Compounding his troubles, in August 1974 Onassis's only daughter, Christina, attempted suicide in London, purportedly over a man, but her mental health had been an issue for some time. The next month, September, brought another painful stretch. Aristotle Onassis had checked into a New York hospital under the pseudonym "Phillips" for further tests for a disease called myasthenia gravis (which literally means "serious muscle weakness"). Doctors gave him six months to a year to live. Knowing the end was near, he quietly discharged himself and flew to Skorpios—alone. In October, Onassis's ex-wife, Tina, remarried and died—supposedly of a barbiturate overdose. Onassis had married her when she was a teenager and he was in his forties, and despite the couple's vicious fights and his flagrant affairs, particularly the passionate and long-lasting one with Callas, he still considered Tina his "true" wife over Jackie. Although an accidental death was a likely scenario given Tina's addictions, these circumstances were also suspicious, but her husband, Onassis's shipping rival Stavros Niarchos, was not charged. (Niarchos's previous wife, Tina's sister, had also died of suspicious causes, but he was not charged then, either.)

Onassis's family was not the only thing falling apart. His business enterprises were struggling, in part due to the Middle East's oil embargo with America, which directly reduced tanker traffic. On top of that, local residents in New Hampshire had just blocked his plans for an oil refinery there. And after nearly twenty years of ownership, he was being forced to turn over Olympic Airways and its thirty jets to the Greek government, due in part to the global economic crisis and rising fuel prices, which led to austerity measures and a pilot strike, halting all flights[26] to five continents as the company lost tens of millions of dollars.[27] His dreams for turning Haiti into the next Monaco had collapsed. And only a fraction of the apartments in his 250-unit Olympic Tower in New York had been sold despite an expensive advertising campaign. By November 1974, Onassis was back in the New York hospital using the same pseudonym. Christina, clinging to her sole surviving immediate family member, was by his side. Jackie was not.

She had given Onassis more prestige than money could buy. She had tolerated his tantrums and flagrant infidelity with Callas, embarrassingly displayed in front-page photos of them together in Paris. It was easier for Jackie to stay married to him because there was often an ocean between them: he in Europe, she in her comfortable Manhattan apartment at 1040 Fifth Avenue, where she had moved a year after the assassination. The fifteen-room apartment, a few blocks from her sister's, had been constant and comfortable as a family base over the last six years while she was shuttling back and forth between Athens, Skorpios, Paris, and New York—between a needy husband and school-aged children.

By now, however, the distance between Jackie and Onassis had never been greater—even though they were, at the moment, in the same city. When he checked out of the hospital, he had a few pieces of business to attend to in Manhattan.

On December 3, Onassis had lunch in Midtown at 21—the same storied restaurant where JFK dined shortly before his inauguration—with Bobby's old boss, Roy Cohn. Cohn, a ruthless lawyer, was now in private practice, and Onassis was asking him to begin divorce proceedings.[28] Not long after, Onassis also secretly met with *Washington Post* gossip columnist Jack Anderson for lunch at La Caravelle. Onassis sat slumped at the table wearing dark glasses, trying to plant a story about how awful Jackie was; it was a high-stakes agenda with no immediate outcome. Onassis was either too subtle with Anderson, or the story was not good enough for the gossip columnist to write immediately after they spoke. "He had little to say about his famous wife," Anderson would later divulge, "except for a mild complaint about her extravagance and her horsy friends."[29]

Although Onassis did not know it at the time, the meeting with Anderson would be his last with a reporter. His nasty business done, Onassis returned to Athens, leaving Jackie behind in New York.

On New Year's Eve, Onassis was at his apartment in Paris, seriously ill but entertaining his own circle of friends as 1975 dawned. Jackie, in New York, tried to be in a celebratory mood, but she was keenly aware that her marriage was likely to end in divorce or Onassis's death, bringing many dramatic changes and opportunities. That night, she brought her children—each wearing formal clothes—to a Broadway opening, where they were met by the flash of paparazzi. Jackie smiled broadly without looking directly at the camera. If she was upset by the deteriorating condition of Onassis or her marriage, she did not show it at the theater. In many ways, she was at her best under the worst circumstances.

Onassis, meanwhile, skipped champagne that night and opted instead for whiskey and water to soothe his bleeding gums. Knowing this might be his last such occasion, he handed out gifts to his closest associates—including a worthless share of a deal to redevelop Haiti as a gambling destination—to his oldest and closest friend, Costa Gratsos.[30]

Jackie attends a Broadway opening with her children to celebrate the new year, 1975. (*Robin Platzer/Twin Images/Time Life Pictures/Getty Images*)

With the holidays over, Jackie and her children headed to Europe—not to be with Onassis, but to ski at Crans-sur-Sierre, in the heart of the Swiss Alps.[31] Photographers buzzed around the slopes, watching her fall into a split; John gave the paparazzi the finger.

Jackie was back in New York by early January and jumped right into society functions, attending the American Ballet Theatre's thirty-fifth anniversary celebration at City Center. Mikhail Baryshnikov was onstage and he attended the after-party with

Jackie, Caroline, and Lee's daughter, Tina. Lee's marriage had ended the previous July and since then, as a woman who had never worked, she had been searching for a purpose. She had given acting a try, had published the scrapbook *One Special Summer*, did a stint interviewing people for a TV talk show, and was working on her memoirs. But mostly, Lee occupied herself with big social events, such as a fund-raiser for the Lenox Hill Neighborhood House on January 4. She and Jackie arrived at the event together, dressed in leather coats and boots, to see the auction of an oil portrait that William Draper had painted of JFK in 1962.[32]

In addition to her society functions, Jackie was busy moving her belongings out of a house in Peapack, New Jersey, that she had rented as a weekend getaway. Now she had her own country retreat—a converted barn she had recently bought for $200,000 in nearby Bernardsville, in the north-central area of New Jersey. Only her name—not Onassis's—was on the deed. Jackie had called William Doyle, a New York auctioneer, to help her discard the second-home things she no longer wanted. Doyle agreed to take some of John's nursery furniture, JFK's wooden chair with a golden Choate School emblem on the backrest, a table that her mother-in-law, Rose Kennedy, had given them as newlyweds, and a five-foot-high mirror with a carved wooden frame.[33]

"I wish you'd take more," she told Doyle as he paid her $2,000. "What's left I'm going to give to the thrift shop."[34]

But the rest truly was junk. An auction house staff member bought the Choate chair for $300 for his grandson. John Jr.'s antique pine desk fetched $175.[35] In total, the items sold for about $3,000.

With her second husband (who was worth nearly $500 million) on the verge of death, gossips began to wonder if Jackie was reselling clothes and furniture to stockpile cash—like a typical child of the Depression—in case Onassis died and cut her out of his will. But cleaning house and preparing for a new beginning felt good. Jackie was rediscovering the things she loved, hidden for too long behind mounds of history. It was time to dust them off and take them out of the shadows.

CHAPTER TWO

The Writer

M r. Shawn?" she breathed into the phone. "This is Jacqueline Onassis."

William Shawn was the legendary editor of *The New Yorker* magazine, arguably the most competitive literary outlet in which a writer could be published. He was surprised to hear Jackie's voice on the other end of his office phone explaining that she had an idea for an article.

Although Jackie may not have known it, and may not have cared if she did, it was an audacious act for her to call him. Shawn was famously shy and many of the world's most renowned writers knew better than to invade his solitude with an unsolicited query. In fact, Shawn preferred speaking to a writer's secretary rather than have to deal with the person directly.

But Shawn rose to the occasion and agreed to have lunch with her in the fall of 1974 at La Caravelle, then a four-star restaurant considered to be Manhattan's best, a place that JFK's father enjoyed so much that its chef trained and handpicked the one for the Kennedy White House.[1] The restaurant—with a pastel dining room staffed with solicitous captains serving roast duck, soufflés, and martinis—was a favorite of Jackie's because other celebrities didn't gawk at her and the staff gave her the privacy she craved. In fact, the quiet setting was a gift for both of them because Shawn also spoke in a whisper.

Jackie picked lightly over her lunch the way thin women do—a little bit nervous, no doubt, given the task before her—and suggested an article on the new International Center for Photography and its executive director, Cornell Capa, former photographer for *Life*, a magazine whose cover Jackie had already graced three times. Capa had photographed Kennedy's presidential campaign, capturing some of its most memorable events, and had done a book on JFK's first hundred days in the White House. He had helped create Camelot. Shawn said he was interested in the photographer's latest endeavor. And then Jackie took the conversation one step further, pitching Shawn on writing regularly for the magazine.[2] She had been a faithful reader of the magazine's Talk of the Town section and proposed being a contributor. As the waiters came and went, she looked him in the eye and told him that she knew about a lot of things, but especially she knew people. She had met lots of them, from all walks of life.[3]

Shawn, who was highly formal, addressed her as Mrs. Onassis and said he was willing to see her work. Although it may have been a stretch for Shawn to accept a piece from anyone else with such thin experience—celebrity aside—the assignment was a natural fit for Jackie. For one thing, she knew a lot about photography, from both sides of the lens. She had made her first paycheck with a camera. And as part of the Kennedy family, which cultivated its image through photographic sessions on the beach in Hyannis Port, in the Oval Office, or around the Christmas tree in Palm Beach, allowing access for legendary photographers such as Richard Avedon, Jacques Lowe, and Capa, she understood the power of pictures. On top of that, she had always been a good writer, even drafting poems as a little girl. The craft of writing, especially about topics she loved, was good therapy, long overdue for a woman who had stifled her literary instincts for nearly two decades.

Words and books, like money and horses, were central in Jackie's life from the very beginning. She was born on July 28, 1929—a few months before the stock market crash that precipitated the Great Depression—in East Hampton, Long Island, where both sets of grandparents had summer homes. Jackie's sister, Lee, was born in 1933. Before Jackie was five, her stockbroker father, John Vernou Bouvier III (called "Black Jack" and occasionally "the Sheik"[4] because of his tanned skin, dark wavy hair, and ways with women), had lost his fortune. His bank account was so depleted that he had to ask his father-in-law, James T. Lee, for a loan to make ends meet. Instead of loaning him a great deal of money, Lee allowed Black Jack and the family to live rent free in a large duplex at 740 Park Avenue, the luxury co-op apartment building Mr. Lee had just built but in which he still had many vacancies as a result of the Depression.[5] Jackie's horse-riding, chain-smoking, and insecure mother, the volatile Janet Norton Lee, was irate not just at her husband's financial instability but also by his serial philandering—often right under her nose. But Jackie adored her father despite his being a cad, a trait she later seemed willing to accept in her own marriages.

By 1940, Jackie's parents were going through a bitter, public divorce that Manhattan society columns relished reporting. After the split, Black Jack moved into a room at the Westbury Hotel. On Sundays he would toot a special horn signal from his convertible when it was time to pick up Jackie and Lee. Perhaps because he had no sons, or because his daughters were adventurous spirits, he encouraged them to climb trees, ride a handle-free bike, play in the outdoor sculling seats at Columbia University, or watch baseball tryouts there. When the activities made them hungry, he treated them to predinner sweets, like pistachio ice cream.[6] When Jackie wanted a pet rabbit, he indulged her by allowing it to live in the bathtub in his Park Avenue apartment.[7]

Whether he was instilling or nurturing their rebellious spirits, Black Jack soon saw some familiar traits, especially in Jackie, who looked very much like her father. In the first grade at the Chapin School in New York, Jackie was regularly sent to the principal, Miss Stringfellow, and when Janet found out about the disciplinary action she asked her daughter what was going on.

"What happens when you're sent to Miss Stringfellow?" Janet pressed one day while walking home from Central Park.

"Well, I go to her office and Miss Stringfellow says, 'Jacqueline, sit down. I've heard bad reports about you.' I sit down. Then Miss Stringfellow says a lot of things—but I don't listen." [8]

Miss Stringfellow made it her mission to bring the girl in line, telling her, "I know you love horses and you yourself are very much like a beautiful thoroughbred. You can run fast. You can have staying power. You're well built and you have brains. But if you're not properly broken and trained, you'll be good for nothing. Suppose you owned the most beautiful race horse in the world. What good would he be if he wasn't trained to stay on the track, to stand still at the starting gate, to obey commands? He wouldn't even pull a milk truck or a trash cart. He would be useless to you and you would have to get rid of him." [9]

It was an analogy that Jackie, who spent most weekends in equestrian gear, even winning her first fashion prize for coordinating her jodhpurs and cravat, could understand. The words penetrated and many years later, after she had become First Lady, Jackie would credit Miss Stringfellow as being the "first, great moral influence" on her life. [10]

In 1942, Janet remarried, to the gentle and twice-divorced

Hugh D. ("Uncle Hughdie") Auchincloss II, whose grandfather was a founder of Standard Oil. Hughdie already had a smattering of kids: a son, Hugh D. III, nicknamed Yusha, from one ex-wife; another son, Tommy, and a daughter, Nina, as well as a stepson—an aspiring writer named Gore Vidal—from another ex-wife. Janet and Hughdie went on to have two children of their own, "Little Janet" and Jamie. In the summer of 1942, the blended family moved from New York City into Merrywood, his neo-Georgian estate in McLean, Virginia. That property, on a hill with forty-six acres of woods near the Potomac, was complete with a swimming pool, an enclosed badminton court, and a small stable.[11]

Starting the next year, the family spent their summers at Auchincloss's other property, the twenty-eight-room shingled "cottage" called Hammersmith Farm in Newport, Rhode Island, the Gatsbyesque community that had its own tight-knit high society, much like the Hamptons. The Gilded Age mansions built by the bank, steel, and railroad barons were monuments to money and power, and constant reminders of the enduring appeal of both.

Given the upscale path she was on, Jackie was enrolled in Miss Porter's, a finishing school in Farmington, Connecticut. It was one of the obvious choices for prep schools for young women at the time. Jackie flourished there, joining students in boosting the 1944 presidential campaign of Thomas Dewey, the Republican challenging FDR. She dutifully enrolled in the drama club, and whenever she could, rode her horse, which she had convinced her grandfather to send up to her. But her literary life was what truly blossomed at Miss Porter's. She wrote for the school newspaper, the *Salmagundy*, and earned a literary prize in her senior year for "consistency of effort and achievement." The award should not have been surprising. Jackie was always a precocious reader and writer even by age six, when one day, she remarked, "Mummy, I liked the story of the lady and the dog." Her mother, momentarily confused, discovered that instead of napping, Jacqueline had been reading a book of Chekhov's short stories, their sophisticated plots and names no problem for the girl's comprehension.

"Did you understand all the words?" Janet asked.

"Yes—except what's a midwife?"

"Didn't you mind all those long names?"

"No, why should I mind?" [12]

By age eight, Jackie was writing sophisticated poetry, such as this one on Christmas:

Reindeer hooves will soon be drumming/On the roof tops loud and clear . . .[13]

By eleven, she had read *Gone with the Wind* three times.[14] Her grandfather encouraged her to write—as he often wrote to her—and once, when she was twelve, she asked him to edit a poem.

"My dear Jacqueline," he wrote in response, "Holy Writ informs us that it was a futile labor to paint the lily white, and it is equally fatuous for me to attempt the perfecting of the perfect, in any suggested emendations to your delightful lines."[15]

But Jackie was not encouraged only by her grandfather. Her father also pushed her to excel in school.

"I do so, Jackie, want you to be a standout at school. In fact, I've such high ambitions for you," Black Jack wrote to her at Miss Porter's. "I know you've got it in you to be a leader. But what's more, I know you've 'got what it takes' to make your schoolmates like and admire you . . . Just make it come out and show them."

Jackie's mother also saw the girl's academic potential and labeled her daughters accordingly. "Jacqueline is the intellectual one, and Lee will have twelve children and live in a rose-covered cottage," Lee remembered her mother saying.[16]

Jackie's love of words and art blossomed, and fed her academics at Miss Porter's, a venerable training ground for women in a man's world. There, her favorite classes were art history, literature, and English. Her average grade was an A-, but the headmaster always told her parents she could do better. She was still mischievous, dumping a pie in a teacher's lap on a dare, stealing cookies from the kitchen for herself and her roommate, Nancy "Tuck" Tuckerman, who would play an important role later in Jackie's life, as her White House social secretary.

On weekends, Jackie would sometimes visit her nearby uncle Wilmarth "Lefty" Lewis (her stepfather's brother-in-law),[17] an impossibly intellectual literary scholar whose specialties were the romantic poet William Blake and the father of gothic fiction Horace Walpole. She'd browse his rare book library and often received an art book for Christmas from him.[18]

But while she thirsted for information, she often tried to hide her intelligence, especially around men. Once, at a Yale football game, when it was fourth down and five yards to go, she turned to her friend Jonathan Isham and said, "Oh, why are they kicking the ball?"

"Come on, Jackie, none of that," he said, believing she probably knew more about football than he did.[19]

Arthur Schlesinger, Kennedy's presidential historian who spent a significant amount of time with her at Hyannis Port, watched her intently read books such as *Remembrance of Things Past*. "I realized that, underneath a veil of lovely inconsequence, she concealed a tremendous awareness, an all-seeing eye and a ruthless judgment."[20]

In her Farmington graduation yearbook, Jackie defined her "ambition" as "never to be a housewife." Although she likely meant the remark as a rebellion from the presumption of a stultifying bourgeois life—her family had enough money to ensure she would probably never be doing her own vacuuming or cooking—the sentiment was the opposite of what most young women then aspired to.

As Jackie prepared to graduate from Miss Porter's, all around her she saw what Betty Friedan would later confirm in *The Feminine Mystique*: a postwar plunge in women going to college. In fact, the proportion of women attending college in comparison with men dropped from 47 percent in 1920 to

35 percent in 1958. The women who applied to universities seemed to be there until they found husbands, as Jackie's sister, Lee, did with her first marriage to Michael Canfield. Some women even thought getting too much of an education would be a hindrance to marriage. Colleges built dormitories for married students, with the wives working toward a "Ph.T."— putting husband through.[21]

Jackie still considered secondary education an important goal. She scored in the ninetieth percentile on the college entrance exams and was off to Vassar, the all-girls college in New York's Hudson Valley, right after her debutante party at Hammersmith Farm, with no fewer than three hundred guests. Cholly Knickerbocker, the famous Hearst columnist and brother of fashion designer Oleg Cassini, summed her up in a headline: QUEEN DEBUTANTE OF THE YEAR 1947.

After her first year at Vassar, Jackie traveled to Europe with three friends and a teacher on the *Queen Mary* and attended a royal garden party at Buckingham Palace, where they shook hands with Winston Churchill. They then toured chateau country in France, and made their way through Milan, Venice, Florence, and Rome. She was enthralled.[22]

Jackie enjoyed what she was learning at Vassar, later saying that "all my greatest interests—in literature and art, Shakespeare and poetry—were formed because I was fortunate enough to find superb teachers in these fields."[23] But Poughkeepsie was a sharp contrast with Europe. She grew restless and applied for a junior-year-abroad program in France, where she lived with a family in Grenoble before heading to the Sorbonne. (Her friend Letitia "Tish" Baldrige, three years ahead of her at Miss Porter's, was working at the French embassy at that time.) There, Jackie took a photography course, and soaked up the language. She loved France. But she also missed her homes, which to her had their own souls, memories, secrets, and stories. They were places that embodied and nurtured her life.

"I always love it so at Merrywood—so peaceful—with the river and the dogs—and listening to the Victrola," she wrote to her stepbrother Yusha from the Sorbonne. "I will never know which I love best—Hammersmith with its green fields and summer winds—or Merrywood in the snow—with the river and those great steep hills. I love them both—whichever I'm at—just as passionately as I loved the one I left behind."[24]

When the school year was over, she stretched her European travels through the summer and then, not wanting to return to campus in New York, enrolled at George Washington University, close to Merrywood.

"Most of my friends had left Vassar to get married," Jackie later explained. "And I wanted to be closer to my family, who were living in Washington."[25]

One day, at Merrywood, Janet was flipping through the pages of *Vogue* and came across a writing contest—the Prix de Paris. She tore out the notice and sent it to Jackie, urging her, between her studies at GWU, to enter. "It's something you'd do well and find amusing," Janet said encouragingly.[26]

After surviving an initial round of *Vogue* judging, Jackie sat down and typed, with only a few grammatical errors, twenty pages of finalist material, including a plan for an entire issue built around the theme "nostalgia," which described clothes that she would soon be famous for wearing. In response to the call for five hundred words on "People I Wish I Had Known," including favorite people in "art, literature or other milieus, no longer living," she named the French poet Charles Baudelaire, the British author and playwright Oscar Wilde, and the Russian ballet dancer Sergei Diaghilev, whose famed Ballets Russes George Balanchine had choreographed in the 1920s.[27]

"If I could be a sort of Overall Art Director of the Twentieth Century, watching everything from a chair hanging in space, it is their theories of art that I would apply to my period, their poems that I would have music and paintings and ballets composed to. And they would each make good stepping stones if we thought we could climb any higher," she wrote.

She also told the magazine that it should not abandon its mix of drawings, models, and celebrities to show off clothes, because without such visual variety "*Vogue* would be a bore if it offered nothing but poker faced mannequins posturing through its pages. It would have the commercial deadliness of some wholesale buyers [*sic*] magazine. It is fun to come across Marlene Dietrich brooding in a great cape or Mrs. R. Fulton Cutting II sitting in a pink cloud of William Winkler nylon tulle," she said.[28]

For her self-portrait part of the entry, she wrote that she has:

. . . a square face and eyes so unfortunately far apart that it takes three weeks to have a pair of glasses made with a bridge wide enough to fit over my nose. I do not have a sensational figure but can look slim if I pick the right clothes. I flatter myself on being able at times to walk out of the house looking like a poor man's Paris copy, but often my mother will run up to inform me that my left stocking seam is crooked or the right-hand topcoat button is about to fall off. This, I realize, is the Unforgiveable Sin. I lived in New York City until I was 13 and spent summers in the country. I hated dolls, loved horses and dogs and had skinned knees and braces on my teeth for what must have seemed an interminable length of time to my family.

I read a lot when I was little, much of which was too old for me. There were Chekov [sic] and Shaw in the room where I had to take naps and I never slept but sat on the window sill still reading, then scrubbed the soles of my feet so the nurse would not see I had been out of bed. My heroes were Byron, Mowgli, Robin Hood, Little Lord Fauntleroy's grandfather, and Scarlett O'Hara.

On men's fashion, she wrote that *Vogue* should direct their coverage toward educating women on the subject, because they did the buying. She said the articles should explain what is a "sack back" jacket, show various collar types, how to "convert" men to wear French cuffs, and why a guy should have a pair of suspenders with every set of pants "so he won't have to switch them when he is in a hurry." "Tell women that well-dressed men are bound by convention and good taste to a limited field," she wrote, "but that within this field a great deal can be done to obtain color, variety and elegance."[29]

Another feature she wrote as part of the contest entry proposed pictures of perfume bottles shot next to close-ups of famous noses. As an alternative, she suggested bottles set next to open books, accompanied by quotes from Milton, Oscar Wilde, and Shakespeare such as:

> *A violet in the youth of primy nature*
> *Forward, not permanent sweet, not lasting*
> *The Perfume and suppliance of a minute.*
>
> —*Shakespeare*, Hamlet

She showed her own literary flair in another part of her *Vogue* submission, a fictional short story—ominously about a wake, the death of her grandfather, during which a friend of the deceased places violets on the coffin. When the visitor leaves, a relative huffs that the violets do not belong there, and moves them to the floor. Jackie wrote:

> *I picked up the violets and put them to my face. They smelled cool and raindrops were still on them . . . I knelt on the bench beside the coffin and put the violets down inside, beneath my grandfather's elbow, where the people who came too close the coffin would not see them.*[30]

The Prix de Paris's winner would be entitled to a year working as a junior editor—six months in the Paris office and six months in the New York office. Jackie won first prize out of 1,280 entrants from 225 colleges. Winning meant she would report to *Vogue* in September 1951, after graduation from George Washington with a degree in French literature.

First, however, she would spend the summer traveling in Europe with Lee, who had just completed high school. The sisters boarded the *Queen Elizabeth*, and immediately began documenting their trip with a scrapbook of their mischievous adventure. They called it *One Special Summer*, wrote it in longhand, and embellished it with drawings—Jackie had a talent there, too—as well as snapshots and flowery handwriting. The scrapbook, rediscovered many years later in an attic by Lee when she was sorting through memorabilia for a book she was writing, was eventually published in 1974, "without a word or penstroke changed," according to the dust jacket.

"We split the fun," Lee wrote in the forward. "Jackie did the drawings, the poetry and the parts on Rome and Spain. I described most of our adventures—on the *Queen Elizabeth*, in London, Paris, Venice, Rome and Florence."

Jackie's poems, like the one below from the scrapbook, had become wittier with time, and her French was excellent.

I danced a gavotte
I ate an éclair
I looked for Lee
But she wasn't there
"Mais vous navez pas vu ma petite soeur?

37

Elle est si jeune—j'ai un peu peur" *
Yes she's taking the air
With Monsieur Moliere

I did minuets
I drank champagne
Looking for Lee
Always in vain
"Mais vous navez pas vu ma petite soeur?
Elle est si jeune—j'ai un peu peur"
Oh she's behind the trees
With the Duc de Guise [31]

Aside from the wonderful memories—and charming book—the trip had a profound impact on Jackie in ways that she may not fully have understood until almost a quarter century later. Late in their trip, in Venice, the sisters dropped in on Bernard Berenson, a legendary art historian who had grown up in Boston, attended Harvard, and written volumes of criticism. He had served as an adviser to Isabella Stewart Gardner, helping her buy European art that hangs on the walls of her villa-museum in Boston today.

The meeting with Berenson was an occasion at least three years in the making. At fifteen, Lee had written to him from Miss Porter's, where she had become immersed in Italian Re-

---

* The sentence means: "But you have not seen my sister? She is so young, I'm scared."

naissance art history. When he replied to her note, she was determined to meet him. As he lounged, wearing a three-piece suit and tie, in a well-stuffed upholstered chaise, propped up by a velvet pillow with a madonna-and-child oil painting hanging on the wall behind him in his sitting room, Berenson told the sisters: "Never follow your sense—marry someone who will constantly stimulate you—and you him." Indeed, what the white-bearded man with hands like "silky polished marble" and a brown hat said to them on their grand tour seemed profound, telling them there are two kinds of people—those who are "life diminishing" and those who are "life enhancing."

And then he told them, "The only way to exist happily is to love your work."

Lee was moved by the meeting. "He has loved and loves beautiful women and beautiful things and above all his work," she wrote in the scrapbook, "which is the one thing that makes life worthwhile and complete . . . We left almost feeling depressed as our visit had seemed so incomplete. We had hardly said a word and every word of his was so great and so true that if we only could have listened longer—then gone away and contemplated all of it, and choose the path from there. He set a spark burning. It was the difference between living and existing that he had spoken of and both of us had simply been existing in our own selfish ways for far too long. Maybe that was why it was so upsetting but more because you longed to reap out of life what he had but knew you never could." [32]

Later in life, Jackie would remember Berenson as one of the

two most impressive men she had ever met.[33] (The other was Charles de Gaulle.)

After feeding pigeons in Saint Mark's Square and getting a taste for the good life's long lunches at outdoor cafés, her first days on the job at *Vogue* in New York were not what Jackie expected. Her special desk was next to editor Bettina Ballard. She was dark haired and stern looking, like a mother bird perched in her big pale-green office at the end of a long hallway on the nineteenth floor of New York's Graybar Building. Jackie watched various editors pay homage to Ballard, and propose ideas for photo shoots or a story.[34]

"Bettina, dahling, thees is you!" one affected male editor said, dramatically draping some sage-green velvet over Ballard's desk.[35] Jackie quit. Neither Shakespeare nor an eligible bachelor was in sight. In fact, in her *Vogue* entry, she had written that after she had spent a summer in Paris the first time, she realized she "should not be ashamed of a real hunger for knowledge, something I had always tried to hide."

She disguised the reasons for her resignation in a letter to *Vogue*, blaming it on her mother "feeling terrifically strongly about keeping me 'in the home' [in Virginia] . . . But I would rather work at what interests me than have a home base and so we have reached a compromise. I will stay here next fall—and learn to type I guess—and then in January if I still want to work for *Vogue* I can move to New York."[36]

Jackie settled into Washington looking for another job. "Real journalism" seemed a better fit than fashion editing especially for someone who would later publicly admit to having dreamed of writing the great American novel.[37] And she knew it would be good training. For help, she called her stepfather, Hughdie, who, in turn, called his friend Arthur Krock, Washington bureau chief of the *New York Times*. Krock, who was also rumored to help Joe Kennedy "fix" stories in the press and get paid for that work,[38] picked up the phone and dialed Frank Waldrop, the editor of the *Washington Times-Herald*, which was then the most popular paper in the capital.

"Are you still hiring little girls?" Krock asked.

Although journalism was then a man's world, there were certain types of low-wage jobs—like covering society teas and reporting on fashion—that women of Jackie's pedigree were hired to do, often still being financially supported by their parents. The *Times-Herald* in particular had a reputation for hiring attractive young women.[39]

Waldrop wanted to hear more of what Krock had to say.

"Well, I have a wonder for you. She's round-eyed, clever and wants to go into journalism. Will you see her?" Krock asked.[40]

They agreed to have her come in for an interview, meeting first with city editor, Sid Epstein.

"I want to be a reporter," she told Epstein.[41]

"We only hire experienced people," he said.

"I'm also a photographer and used a Leica at the Sorbonne."

Epstein laughed at the combination of her sophistication and naïveté.

"Kid, we don't have anything that fancy."

But Epstein looked at this beautiful young woman and told her the paper could use a new "inquiring photographer," a person to snap headshots and invent questions posed to a handful of people on the street. The position was about to be vacated by a stringer leaving for law school.

"If you can use a Speed Graphic by tomorrow, I'll hire you," he told her. The column would need to be renamed as the Inquiring Camera Girl.

Epstein assigned a staff photographer to help her with such

Jackie in her first job, as the "Inquiring Camera Girl" at the *Washington Times-Herald*. *(Copyright unknown, courtesy of JFK Library)*

things as understanding what the best distance would be to snap head shots. The photographer, six feet tall, lay on the ground and had her stand at his feet so she could gauge the proper spacing.[42]

Jackie came back the next day to meet with Waldrop.

"Do you want to go into journalism, or do you want to hang around here until you get married?" he asked her in his office shortly before Christmas 1951.

"No, sir! I want to make a career!"

"Well, if you're serious, I'll be serious. If not, you can have a job clipping things."

"No, sir! I'm serious."

"OK, then come in after the holidays. But don't you come back to me in six months and say you're engaged!"

"No, sir!"[43]

At the time, Jackie was dating John Husted, a tall blond Yale graduate who had fought in the war, worked on Wall Street, and whose sister had gone to Farmington with Jackie. Husted's social-register family was friendly with Black Jack, as well as Hughdie.

But when she arrived in the newsroom just after the New Year to begin her $42.50 per week job,[44] Waldrop was surprised by her confession.

"I guess you won't want to hire me," she said. "I did get myself engaged over the holidays."

"How long have you known the guy?" Waldrop asked.

"Just a few weeks," she said.

"That won't last!"[45]

Jackie dove into work, asking a topical question of eight to ten people—from housewives to Senate pages, cabinet members to congressmen—and recording their answers and photographs for a piece that ran once a week.

Epstein noticed that the column improved immediately. The kid seemed soft-spoken and shy, but she wasn't afraid to go out and talk with people, unlike her predecessor, who would just go into a bar and interview the guy sitting on the first stool.[46]

Outside of work, things were not going as well. Jackie was having second thoughts about marrying Husted.

Louis Auchincloss, a relative of Jackie's, learned of the engagement at a dinner, during which Jackie talked with him about a novel he'd written called *Sybil*—"a sad little girl who has a dull little life," as he described the character.

"That's going to be my life—Sybil Husted," Jackie said.

Auchincloss felt a conviction come over him—the realization that in fact her life would be anything but.[47]

One attendee described their engagement party at Hammersmith as "chilly"—noticeably absent of affection[48]—and at the end of a visit to Merrywood in mid-March, she drove Husted to the airport and slipped the ring into his pocket.[49]

"She didn't say much and neither did I," Husted recalled. "There wasn't much you could say."[50]

What she didn't tell Husted, and what she didn't tell her boss, and what she had even denied to herself, was that she was falling hard for another guy. He was much older, thirty-four.

His name was Jack Kennedy, a congressman from Massachusetts. She had met him at a dinner party in Georgetown the year before, in 1950, at the home of Charles Bartlett, Washington correspondent for the *Chattanooga Times*. After dinner, Kennedy followed Jackie and her host out to the car and "muttered shyly," according to Bartlett: "Shall we go someplace and have a drink?" But Jackie couldn't join him because as she approached her car, there was already another young man—a "friend"— waiting for her in the backseat; he had climbed in unexpectedly after seeing her car. Jack saw him and backed off.[51] But shortly after she was engaged to Husted, whom Bartlett said "didn't seem worthy of her hand," Bartlett's wife, Martha, was hosting a party that Husted could not attend and told Jackie to invite someone else: Jack.[52]

Who could blame her for falling for the young senator-elect? Tall, thin, with a mop of reddish-brown hair and blue eyes, he was a Harvard graduate and war hero. He was intellectually curious, outgoing, and exuded animal magnetism, always seeming to draw women to him. He was an eligible bachelor and had successfully crisscrossed Massachusetts to unseat the entrenched Senator Henry Cabot Lodge.

Jackie's romantic angst was evident in her journalism, where she processed her deepest fears, insecurities, and anxieties about the cultural expectation that a woman of her age (just twenty-two) and education should already be married. And perhaps because of her own parents' divorce, she also seemed worried about losing herself to a man—or choosing the wrong one.

"What do you think women desire most?" she probed in one of her columns.

"A Boston University professor said women should marry because they're too lazy to go to work," began another column.

Jackie also wrote about politics. After the 1952 Republican convention, she went to Tilden Street in DC and asked residents—including family members—what they thought of Senator Nixon, who lived there.

"He's always away," said six-year-old Tricia Nixon. "If he's famous why can't he stay home? See this picture? That's a coming home present I made for Daddy. Julie did one, too, but she can't color as well as me. All my class was voting for Eisenhower, but I told them I was just going to vote for Daddy."[53]

A year into the job, she covered President Eisenhower's inaugural parade, writing about it but also drawing charming pen-and-ink cartoons of the crowds. At the end of the article, Jackie described Vice President Nixon as "wilting considerably more than Eisenhower"[54] after the walk, a prescient comment seven years before Nixon would break into a sweat during a famous presidential debate with JFK.

A few months after the inaugural column, Waldrop told her to interview people who were recently elected, including Jack Kennedy, who had beaten Lodge for the Senate. Waldrop knew and liked Kennedy and had heard that Jack and Jackie had been seeing each other. Without telling Jackie that, he lectured her about him, warning that Kennedy "doesn't want to get married."[55]

"This bird [Kennedy] is older than you and far more experienced," he said. "Mind your step."

"Yes, sir," she said, rolling her eyes.[56]

When she told Kennedy that she needed to interview him, he told her to question him after all the others, giving him the advantage of the last word.

The column, which appeared on April 21, 1953, asked the young, boyish-looking Senate pages what they thought of the senators and then asked the senators—Kennedy and Richard Nixon, who had just moved from the Senate to vice president—about the pages. The interviewees' mug shots faced each other on opposite columns, their words completing the contrast between the young and more personable Kennedy and the older, stiff, and long-winded Nixon. The whole column was a bizarre prelude: here was JFK's future wife interviewing Nixon, his opponent in the 1960 presidential campaign.

"I would predict that some future statesman will come from the ranks of the page corps," Nixon told her. "During my time as a senator I noticed that they were very quick boys, most of whom have a very definite interest in politics and feel that they could not get a better political grooming than by witnessing the Senate in session day after day as they do."

Kennedy was more playful in his answer for the Inquiring Camera Girl. "I've often thought that the country might be better off if we Senators and pages traded jobs. If such legislation is ever enacted, I'll be glad to hand over the reins to Jerry Hoobler," he said referring to his seventeen-year-old page. "In the meantime, I think he might be just the fellow to help me straighten out my relationship with the corps. I have often mistaken Jerry for a Senator because he looks so old."

Hoobler said, "Senator Kennedy always brings his lunch in a brown paper bag. I guess he eats it in his office. I see him with it every morning when I'm on the elevator. He's always being mistaken for a tourist by the cops because he looks so young. The other day he wanted to use the special phones and they told him, 'Sorry, mister, these are reserved for senators.'"

Through her columns, Jackie also asked more questions about men, women, and marriage.

> *"Do you think a wife should let her husband think he's smarter than*
> *she is?"*
> *"Chaucer said that what most women desire is power over men.*
> *What do you think women desire most?"*
> *"When did you discover that women are not the weaker sex?"*
> *"Should a candidate's wife campaign with her husband?"*
> *"Which first lady would you most like to have been?"*
> *"Would you like your son to grow up to be president?"*
> And, among her last, *"What is your candid opinion of marriage?"*

Jackie knew she was smart, perhaps even smarter than some of the men she was interviewing. And she had a job. But by midcentury standards, she was thinking that both of these facts were not attributes; they were barriers to marriage. Having already missed the senior-year engagement deadline—the mantra was "a ring by spring"—Jackie was trying not to be unnerved by the passage of time as she attended cocktail parties of the powerful and famous around Washington. In April 1953, Lee had married Michael Canfield, adopted son of Cass Canfield, who was publisher of Harper & Row.

Her mother sensed Jackie's anxiety and urged her to take a trip to England with a family friend. Jackie was reluctant, probably because she did not want to leave Jack, but her mother insisted. Jackie asked Epstein—a newspaper editor who was as gruff as they got—for a two-week vacation in June. He did not mask his annoyance.

"You haven't been on the job long enough to rate a vacation," he snapped.

"But I've been invited to the coronation of the queen," she said, letting her stunning revelation seep in.

Epstein, who had been trying unsuccessfully to get someone into the event, shouted, "Go! But you have to write us letters you airmail back. And include a sketch every day." [57]

She left, quietly longing for a ring from the man she truly loved but excited by the adventure of once again crossing the Atlantic, a trip she called "the Mayflower in reverse" in her report. [58] The Duke and Duchess of Windsor were on the ship—as were their dogs, valet, and maid. "Sometimes the Duke of Windsor takes a turn around the deck in sports jacket and gray flannel trousers," she wrote. "The Windsors are landing at La Havre. They are not going to the coronation. Passengers stare at the Duke, aware that if he had not abdicated, they would not be sailing to the coronation of his niece." Waldrop published her words and sketches on the front page.

Back home, Janet marveled at her daughter's clever drawings and wondered if Jack had seen them. She figured he surely had, since he had been increasingly appreciative of Jackie's talents.[59]

Despite the deadlines and the news in London, Jackie managed to spend time there buying books. She bought so many that she needed a separate suitcase whose weight cost her $100 extra in baggage to ship home. She didn't mind paying the freight. They were a gift to JFK, mostly about history and legislation.[60] When she landed, he picked her up and they headed to the Cape, where Kennedy presented her with a large emerald-and-diamond engagement ring, personally delivered by two men from Van Cleef and Arpels.

And then she did what so many other women at that time in history did when a man asked for her hand. She quit her job. She was twenty-three.[61]

"Who's the lucky guy?" Waldrop asked. When she told him, Waldrop said, "Isn't he a little too elderly for you?" Kennedy was thirty-six. Kidding aside, everyone knew the wedding would be an auspicious event. Waldrop ran the engagement announcement on the front page.

On September 11, 1953, the night before their epic wedding with twelve hundred guests at Hammersmith Farm, JFK, then a freshman senator, toasted his bride by saying he was motivated to marry her because she was so good as the Inquiring Camera

Girl that he needed to remove her from the press corps to save his political future.

She needled him back, holding up a postcard from Bermuda he had sent to her—the only written communication she had received from him while they were dating.

"Wish you were here," he scrawled. "Jack."[62]

The winter after they were married, the Kennedys were settling into a home on Dent Place in Washington. Jackie put her thoughts and drawings on paper for her younger sister. It was called *A Book for Janet: In Case You Are Ever Thinking of Getting Married This Is a Story to Tell You What It's Like.*

One of the pictures she drew was of her waving good-bye to Jack as he left the house in the morning. Another was of the dome of the Capitol all lit up at night, and there was a rhyme underneath it about when you saw the light burning there late at night and Jack wasn't home yet, you knew that the country was safe.[63]

Although she was happy, the early years of their marriage were consumed by Kennedy's grave back problems. Born with one leg shorter than the other, he was also gimpy from aggressive tackling while playing football for Harvard. And then, during World War II, Kennedy had been a lieutenant in the US Navy, at the wheel of a small patrol boat in the Solomon Islands, when a Japanese destroyer sliced through the black of night into his boat, shearing off the starboard side and igniting a fire. Kennedy was slammed into the deck, rupturing a disc in his spinal column. He and five other shipmates hung on to the hull. Kennedy rescued three of the men, floating about a hundred yards away, while others rescued two more mates clustered equally as far in the opposite direction. Still stranded the next day, Kennedy, doing the breaststroke, towed on his back the badly burned and most injured sailor for four hours through three miles of water toward an island so small it had only six coconut trees. The ordeal did not end there. Kennedy swam even more through harsh currents and coral reefs, sometimes with the same injured sailor, looking to be rescued. Finally, days later, they were found by some natives in a canoe.[64] The saga made him a hero and legend, but the damage to his back was done. He was invalided out of the navy and worked as a war correspondent briefly before having the disc removed in 1944.

A decade later, in October 1954, he couldn't even bend over to pick up a piece of paper, didn't want to sit in the car for long stretches, and was hobbling on crutches. Doctors told him he needed a lumbar fusion to save him from life in a wheelchair, and he went under the knife again, to insert a metal plate into his spine. Kennedy also had Addison's disease, which lowered his immunity to infection, and he slipped into a coma after the surgery. A priest delivered last rites. He recovered enough to fly—lying on a stretcher—to Palm Beach to be with his family over Christmas, with Jackie doting on him, even dressing his incision as he lay on his belly for hours, cranky and bored. Jackie mopped his brow, fed him, and helped him out of bed, read aloud to him and recited poems—anything to distract him from the agony. Kennedy had his own favorite poems to reflect on, especially Alan Seeger's "I Have a Rendezvous with Death." [65] But Kennedy's back was not healing, and he needed yet another surgery in February to remove the plate and perform a bone graft. He returned to Palm Beach again to recuperate in a hospital bed that had been set up in a two-room first-floor suite of his father's Spanish-style mansion on the ocean. The living room of the suite had been converted into a study filled with books and cabinets.

Jackie continued her emotional, physical, and intellectual support. Reading him stacks of newspapers to occupy his mind only went so far, as did the games and guests she brought in. Eventually, their discussions floated back to the spring before, when Jackie had enrolled in the Georgetown School of Public Service, taking a class on American history. She recalled that during one class, her professor had lectured dramatically about John Adams's diplomatic courage and pluck, which had averted war with France. Jack, meanwhile, had been intrigued by Adams for some time and the hard choices Adams had made with Boston's economic interests in mind. Early in his Senate career, Kennedy was also focused on his home state's economy and drew inspiration from Adams. The husband and wife agreed there was an idea there—an important story to tell about elected officials who faced down danger or went against popular sentiment to accomplish what they thought was right. In fact, Kennedy had already asked his speechwriter, Ted Sorensen, to begin collecting similar examples of political courage.

Sorensen called Jackie's young Brooklyn-bred professor,

Dr. Jules Davids, to learn more about Adams and he also began pulling records from the Library of Congress. Eventually, after the Kennedys conferred with Lee's husband, Michael Canfield, about writing a piece for *Harper's* magazine, they all realized the idea could be a book with more than a half dozen politicians given their own chapters written as case studies.

"What would the size of a book be?" Kennedy asked the younger Canfield.

"Oh, at least 50,000 words," he replied.

Kennedy called Sorensen and relayed their conversation.

"It's a wonderful idea and I am prepared to work but bear in mind the article we wrote for the Sunday *New York Times* magazine was 1,500 words and it was a lot of work," Sorensen told him. "This would be the equivalent of 33 *New York Times* articles."

Kennedy was undeterred. He and Jackie began doing their part in Palm Beach. She made sure that around his bed were worktables, filing cabinets, a dictating machine, and a telephone. His day would begin with breakfast in bed at 8:00, followed by reading papers from New York, Boston, Miami, and Palm Beach, then the *Congressional Record*, and then the mail.[66] In the afternoon, he'd talk with Sorensen, who visited twice in Palm Beach to move the book project further along, often hauling material from the Library of Congress.[67]

The original manuscript has JFK's handwritten notes, as well as those from Sorensen in the margin.[68] But Jackie's role is undeniable—she was the book's midwife—and she gave the manuscript one final read before it was sent to the publisher.

"The greatest debt is owed to my research assistant, Theodore C. Sorensen, for his invaluable assistance in the assembly and preparation of the material upon which this book is based," Kennedy wrote in the preface to the book, named *Profiles in Courage*. But the final person Jack thanked in the preface—and the person he dedicated the book to—was Jackie. "This book would not have been possible without the encouragement, assistance and criticisms offered from the very beginning by my wife Jacqueline, whose help during all the days of my convalescence I cannot ever adequately acknowledge."

The next year, with Kennedy back on his feet, *Profiles in Courage* won the Pulitzer Prize for biography* and helped ignite his launch for the presidency and perhaps Jackie's interest in editing.[69] But for the moment, Jackie was devoted to another profession: being a smartly coiffed and supportive political wife.

Instead of pursuing others with a notebook and a camera, she was now pursued. While Jack thrived on crowds, she avoided them, instead finding quiet corners to voraciously read novels by Kerouac or Colette, or the memoirs of the Duc de Saint-Simon about life at Versailles, which especially prepared her for life in the White House. During the Wisconsin primary, she read *War and Peace*, two bleak landscapes playing off each other.[70] Even if

---

* *Profiles* was Kennedy's second book. The first was *Why England Slept*, his senior thesis at Harvard about Britain's policies in the years leading up to World War II. Arthur Krock, his friend at the *New York Times*, encouraged him to publish the manuscript, which was about the conflict between democracy and dictatorship and the relationship between leadership and freedom. Published in 1940, it was reprinted when he was president and became a bestseller.

she did not like politics and the fishbowl it forced her to live in, she had great instincts, knowing how to motivate an important demographic, as for example when she addressed a Bronx crowd in Spanish, or how she could inform an important speech by translating French books and documents to help her husband's Senate testimony on Algeria or Indochina.[71]

Aside from adapting to the glare of politics in the early years of her marriage, Jackie was also transformed in another way: she became a mother. After giving birth to a stillborn daughter in August 1956, Caroline was born by cesarean section in November 1957.

Pregnant again—with John Jr.—during the presidential campaign in 1960, her doctors wanted her to take it easy given her obstetrical history. So instead of riding airplanes and shaking hands, she put her writing skills to work again, penning six weekly newspaper columns between September 16 and November 1 called Campaign Wife. The folksy dispatches portrayed what it was like to be married to a man running for president. In effect, the columns were Jackie's way of being public when she was pregnant and unable to travel on the campaign. The columns were issued out of the Democratic National Committee as press releases, at least being honest about what they were.

The first column was about weathering a hurricane in Hyannis Port that knocked down trees and blew off part of the roof. "We really weren't terribly frightened, but Caroline did worry about what was happening to her father and whether her kitten and puppy were safe," Jackie wrote. "Once she was assured Jack was in Texas where there was no storm, and Mitten and Charley were with us, we spent a cozy evening reading stories by candlelight." In the next paragraph, she writes that her doctor allowed her to go to New York for a campaign trip, where she appeared on a TV show, shopped for maternity clothes, and spoke with reporters. "All the talk over what I wear and how I fix my hair has amused and puzzled me," she wrote. "What does my hairdo have to do with my husband's ability to be President?"[72]

In the last column, she could barely contain her excitement. "One more week until November 8th. It's hard to imagine how everyone can keep working at the same pace even seven more days and yet these are the most important days when volunteers across the country are calling to be sure everyone goes to the polls. If everyone is working as hard and the women who have sent in thousands of Calling for Kennedy forms telling what women believe to be the most important issues facing the country Jack and Senator Johnson are sure to be elected!"[73]

All of these writing experiences came rushing back to her in late 1974 as Jackie toiled on the *New Yorker* piece. She took her time reporting it and reviewed her words carefully, knowing that the magazine was just another kind of fishbowl. She put the pages in an envelope and sent the piece by courier to William Shawn's cluttered office at 25 West Forty-Third Street.

How surprisingly good it would feel to have a published article again—in one of the most influential literary magazines in the world—even without her name on it, as the Talk of the Town pieces did not include bylines then. *The New Yorker* was a magazine that had published Dorothy Parker, John Cheever, Truman Capote, Harper Lee, Ring Lardner, W. H. Auden, Vladimir Nabokov, E. B. White, J. D. Salinger, John Updike, and most every other literary light of the twentieth century. It had been a long dry spell from journalism for her, at least as a member of the fourth estate. Of course now she was the object of it, and had been for some time.

When Shawn was done editing her submission, he called her in to discuss the final changes.[74] She could barely see the man seated behind his desk, which was stacked with papers and mail, and contained a glass vase filled with pencils next to a hand-crank sharpener. Behind him, snapshots were tacked to the wall. Her brief visit to the office sent ripples of excitement and curiosity through even the most hardened scribes on staff, who suddenly felt compelled to stretch their legs, gather around the water cooler,[75] and catch a glimpse, all the while imagining what she could have written that he thought was worth publishing.

By mid-January 1975, the Christmas tree was gone from Rockefeller Center but Jackie knew she had one last gift coming to her, and it was waiting in her mailbox. There, rolled up, was the January 13, 1975, issue of *The New Yorker*, in which her Talk of the Town article finally appeared. Upstairs in her apartment, she was thrilled to hold the magazine in her hands, perhaps noting the irony of its cover—a drawing of ladies lunching. The article, spanning four pages, was tucked into the front section. She noted that Shawn had cut the feature in half, to fifteen hundred words, to fit stylistically with the other short pieces.[76] He had also changed Jackie's first-person singular to the magazine's standard "we" and gave it the odd title of "Being Present."

She read her familiar words again, the piece beginning with her description of a lunch at the Met with Karl Katz, whom she called one of the "guiding spirits" behind the photography center, and how they discussed Capa and his humanistic approach to photography. After the lunch, she and Katz had walked up the stretch of Fifth Avenue known as the Museum Mile to Ninety-Fourth Street, and into the historic brick Georgian mansion that had housed the Audubon Society before Capa had located the center there. The piece, she thought, didn't read half bad:

As we stood talking, Mr. Capa walked in—a sturdy man of fifty-six, with bushy hair, bushy eyebrows, and a smiling face. "There you are," he said. "The baby is about to be born. We will make it for the opening. Come I want to show you everything."

Mr. Capa put one arm around Mr. Katz and the other arm around us, and began to steer us through. "We have put the house back exactly as it used to be," he said. "When we moved in there were many partitions, which we have taken down. See the paneling? We will never hurt it. We designed special boards to hang pictures

from, with metal rods." He pointed to a rod that Mr. [Bhupendra]
Karia was holding. "A genius who was produced by Karl Katz
thought these up. But, like all geniuses, he made the rods so that they
wouldn't fit in the holes. Right, Bhupendra?" Mr. Karia smiled.[77]

Although the article was unsigned, it didn't take long before
everyone knew she had written it. The *Washington Post* was so
breathless about her writing the article that the paper immediately reprinted it. *Time* magazine ran an item in its People
column suggesting she wrote it for the paycheck. "Is Jackie Kennedy Onassis going broke?" the magazine asked.[78]

Jackie, slightly bemused by the attention, issued a typically
demure statement through her old classmate and former White
House social secretary, Nancy Tuckerman, which said, "I am
glad *The New Yorker* took my piece if it helps more people to
know about the International Center of Photography."[79]

The reclusive Shawn, of course, was not interested in engag-
ing the press either, though he no doubt understood the value of
having Jackie's name in the magazine, for reasons other than its
literary merit. Rather than deal with each reporter who called,
he, too, released an underwhelming statement, saying the article
"was delivered to us by messenger. It's a straightforward little
piece of reporting, very good and very usable with a little editing . . . She will be paid at the regular rates, which run into the
hundreds rather than the thousands."[80]

Crossing the street from 1040 Fifth for some fresh air in
Central Park, Jackie could see *The New Yorker* on the newsstand,

and if she smiled, it was surely in the knowledge that years after her debutante ball, this literary coming-out party allowed her to unleash a little bit of creativity in a very public way. She had produced something of worth and had been paid for it. She had exposed her passion for art, culture, and preservation, as well as an abiding curiosity about what to do next with her life—things that had been on her mind more lately with her marriage ending and her children verging on adulthood. By publishing, she was asserting herself, reviving her talents, and erecting a bridge to a new land, from one rarified world of glamorous parties, exotic vacations, and a life defined by her husbands to another, where she could express her true self. It had been a long time since she had received a check to publish her work. And it felt good, despite—or perhaps because of—the fact that she was married to one of the richest people in the world. That the piece explored art (photography) as well as architecture (the Audubon House) is not surprising. Surely she knew what Hemingway said: Write what you know.

CHAPTER THREE

The Preservationist

J ackie was home at 1040 Fifth on the morning of January 22, 1975, reading the *Times* over breakfast, when she spotted a story by Paul Goldberger, the paper's young architecture critic. Her eyes locked on the front-page headline: CITY'S NAMING OF GRAND CENTRAL AS A LANDMARK VOIDED BY THE COURT. She hurriedly read the words on the cover and jumped to the rest of the story inside the paper. There, with the article, was a picture of the terminal's facade, with the modernist Pan Am building, completed in 1963, looming over the north side of Grand Central—a stark reminder of how easily the skyline could change for the worse. Jackie was outraged by what she read. She cared about the station. It was a place symbolic of old Manhattan, a city her grandfather had helped build.

Grand Central was one of America's finest examples of Beaux-Arts architecture, which uses classical elements and sculpture in a monumental way. The Beaux-Arts school originated in Paris, where Jackie had seen the style applied at the Opera, the Louvre, and the Grand Palais. In her own city, there was City Hall, the New York Public Library, Carnegie Hall, and the Federal Reserve Bank, to name a few—all inspiring buildings. This was a building, a very democratic one, that she believed was worth keeping. She picked up the phone.

Laurie Beckelman, a twenty-three-year-old part-time office assistant at the Municipal Art Society, was fielding calls as quickly as she could from the moment she walked in. People were alarmed by Goldberger's story, which said that State Supreme Court Justice Irving Saypol had invalidated the landmark status of Grand Central Terminal, making it possible for the station to be redeveloped as an office tower, with the bulk of the new structure plunked on top of or encompassing the old building.

The phone rang again. Beckelman reached for it, expecting this caller to be like all of the others, asking how they could help to save Grand Central.

"May I please speak with Kent Barwick?"

"May I ask who is calling?" Beckelman said, sitting at her wooden desk, which was cluttered with papers and a typewriter in the two-room office on East Sixty-Fifth Street.

"Jacqueline Onassis." [1]

Beckelman's boss, Kent Barwick, was executive director of

the Municipal Art Society (MAS). He had been a copywriter at the global advertising agency BBDO before becoming interested in preservation when three iconic places in New York were threatened with destruction: Fulton Market, the iron facades of SoHo, and, his personal favorite, McSorley's saloon. He was an ardent volunteer at MAS and was eventually asked to lead the group as executive director in spring 1969. Born on suburban Long Island, Barwick's grandparents had lived in New York and when he visited he was always awed by the vision of elegantly dressed men with their briefcases spilling out of Grand Central. But he had no idea his interest in urban landscape and architecture would lead him to this.

"I know you won't believe me," Beckelman shouted to Barwick, a short distance away in his office, with Jackie on hold. "But there's a woman on the phone who claims she's Jackie Onassis."

The only other person working in the cramped space that morning was a young aspiring actress, Laura Korach, and she, like Beckelman, stopped what she was doing and stood up to see Barwick's reaction to the call. After picking up the receiver, Barwick heard the unmistakable voice and signaled with a nod that it really was Jackie.[2]

Grand Central had taken ten years to complete in 1913 at the staggering cost of $65 million. By 1929, the year Jackie was born, 47 million passengers were passing through the station annually.[3] Behind the terminal's Indiana limestone facade was a city within a city, a vast place with vaulted ceilings and a four-sided golden clock in the middle of the main concourse. It was filled with the vibration and bass hum of the trains and the *click-click-click* made by heels scurrying across the Tennessee marble floors and the giant schedule boards telling commuters heading to Connecticut and the Hudson River Valley their track numbers. Around Grand Central's perimeter and underground, there were restaurants and shops convenient for nearby office workers—such as those working at *Vogue*, as Jackie had, in the Graybar building next door.

The station's appearance, as well as its location in the heart of the city, had served as the perfect backdrop for drama. Hitchcock movies were filmed there. Soldiers' funeral processions paraded through. And crowds gathered to catch glimpses of living history shown live on a giant television screen: singer Frank Sinatra, boxer Joe Louis, or a rocket launch, like one during the Kennedy administration. Grand Central was a place where people could catch a train or buy a book, a meal, a stock, a bet, or, indeed, by 1975, drugs or a trick.

In the baby boom years after World War II, the car had become a symbol of American freedom. The suburbs were draining families and revenue from cities, especially New York, and train stations, in their neglect, had become seedy and run-down. Grand Central was no different. It was dangerous and depressing. Its cerulean blue ceiling depicting the zodiac in gold was virtually obscured by nicotine soot. Its windows were partly covered with advertising. Its skylights, painted black during the war, remained so. The building was starved of natural light, making it seem even dirtier. Tenants had stripped storefronts of fanciful entries, making it uglier. The roof leaked.[4] Although Jackie knew there was beauty beneath the grime, Grand Central had become a place that New Yorkers had given up on, ceding its waiting room to homeless people.

As Jackie read the rest of the *Times* story, she saw that Judge Saypol had found that the landmark designation imposed an "economic hardship" on the terminal's owner, Penn Central Railroad. Because landmark designation prevented any major changes, it "constitutes a taking of the property." And taking property without compensating the owner is unconstitutional; it says so in the Fifth Amendment.

The decision was alarming to preservationists, whose efforts were being led by the venerable Municipal Art Society, formed in 1893 by architects, painters, sculptors, and civic leaders to create murals and monuments in the city's public spaces. Inevitably, the group had become engaged in bigger urban issues, successfully calling for the city's first zoning code in 1916, helping to plan the subway lines, and pioneering the Landmarks Preservation Law in 1965. That law was created as a result of the razing two years earlier of Pennsylvania Station, designed by the preeminent Beaux-Arts civic building architects McKim, Mead & White. Not only was Penn Station knocked down, but also many felt insulted by its replacement—the modernist office complex and the hideous squat black steel-and-glass arena called Madison Square Garden.

With Penn Station gone, MAS knew that Grand Central was legitimately threatened. In fact, Penn Station's destruction had been the motivating factor for the city to landmark Grand Central in 1967, in the hopes of saving it.

The railroad had hired Marcel Breuer, the Hungarian-born Bauhaus architect, to design a skyscraper for the terminal site. Breuer, known for his 1920s classic leather and metal tube chair called the Wassily, had two years before completed the Whitney Museum, a showcase for contemporary art and an institution where Jackie was an honorary trustee.[5] Set among traditional limestone and brownstone buildings not far from Jackie's apartment, the Whitney was built out of slabs of gray granite, designed with only a few windows, in the style of brutalism, a form of architecture that aspired to create sculpture out of concrete, but can look as heavy and harsh as it sounds. Breuer had been a leader of the brutalism movement while teaching at Harvard's Graduate School of Design, where his students included Philip Johnson and I. M. Pei. In 1954, Pei had sketched what would have been the tallest structure in the world—a 108-story "hyperboloid" that also would have replaced Grand Central entirely. His proposal, which looked like a slender nuclear reactor with steel webbing on the outside, was rejected.

Breuer was determined to succeed where I. M. Pei had failed and in 1968 he completed his first proposed design for building on top of Grand Central. The plan called for fifty-five stories set on the main terminal, leaving the historic facade intact but destroying its beloved waiting room. The Landmarks Preservation Commission had rejected that proposal. Breuer's next design was for a tower three stories taller, but essentially the same shape, thin and rectangular, like the lid of a shoebox standing on its side. What was different was that the base of the building was supported with posts that dropped over the face of Grand Central like prison bars and would require the demolition of much of the terminal building. The city had denied that proposal as well.

Although the city offered other development sites to the railroad team as a consolation, Penn Central, the railroad that had provided Bobby Kennedy's funeral train from New York to Washington, was struggling financially. And Penn believed that a skyscraper at the Grand Central site was the only way to save itself. The railroad pressed its case in court. And thanks to Judge Saypol, Penn Central—on the brink of bankruptcy—had just won its first round.

In the moments after the judge's decision, Paul Goldberger, the twenty-five-year-old architecture critic, was banging out the story on a manual typewriter with four-ply carbon paper inserted beneath the keys, sitting in his corner of the "culture gulch" section on the tenth floor of the *Times*'s West Forty-Third Street office.[6] Despite the cigarette smoke wafting through the newsroom and the *clanks* and *dings* from the keystrokes around him, Goldberger was focused on what he knew would be big news. And he knew whom to call, as the legal battle had been dragging on for years.

The big question was this: What would the city do in response to Saypol's decision?

Goldberger called Deputy Mayor Stanley Friedman and asked him if the city intended to back down.

"I think we have to appeal—this decision goes to the heart of the landmarks law," Friedman told him.

Goldberger then called Barwick for a quote.

"It is a tragic blow to the government's efforts to make New York a livable city," Barwick said. "We think the public has a basic right to protect the great buildings of the past and we mean to fight for that right."

After he hung up with the reporter, Barwick, fuming over Saypol's decision, huddled with friends and advisers. He was hearing that the railroad was going to try to collect $60 million in damages from the city if officials appealed the case, a devastating thought for politicians at a time when New York was facing a financial collapse of its own for the same reason as the railroad: people were moving out in the midst of an international recession. Barwick was worried that municipal officials—especially New York mayor Abraham Beame, who began his career as an accountant—might lose their resolve to wage an expensive legal fight.

Beame, elected the year before, was struggling with New York's worst fiscal calamity since the Great Depression. After years of overspending combined with declining revenue, the city couldn't pay its bills and was having trouble borrowing to do so. Beame was trying to find ways to slash the budget, which meant firing teachers, fire fighters, and police officers. He had neither the time nor the inclination to worry about spending more money to fight Penn Central. The city coffers were empty, its debts enormous.

After considering all of this, Barwick called Goldberger back, offering a quote that would make it more uncomfortable for Beame to drop the landmark designation.

"We're forming a committee to save the terminal and support the city in its expected appeal," Barwick told him. Goldberger added the information to his story, ripped the carbon book out of his typewriter, turned it in to his editor, and went home, not knowing that the story would move Jackie to call the MAS when it was published the next day.

And here she was, on the phone with Barwick.

"What can I do to help?" Jackie asked.

"We're putting together a committee but the big worry is that Mayor Beame will drop the case," said Barwick. "We're having a press conference. I can imagine how busy your schedule is."

"Well, I'm going to be around," Jackie told him.

"We're thinking of issuing a statement and we can send it to your staff and see if it's something you can support."

"I don't have a staff," Jackie said, not entirely truthfully.

Barwick was shocked. In the backbiting circles of New York society Jackie was known to be virtually unapproachable, as well as domineering in her association with certain circles, like the Metropolitan Museum. Of course, any person with such celebrity would be difficult, Barwick thought. Yet here she was being pleasant, conversational, and professional, offering to do work herself.

Barwick hung up and gave marching orders to Beckelman, who had been part of MAS for two years and was making a $5,500 annual salary. In jeans and a sheepskin coat, the svelte blond headed over to Jackie's apartment to get her signature on a letter that was also signed by architect Philip Johnson, who had become a rival of his old professor, Breuer. The document was the first step to organize an official committee to save Grand Central. A houseboy met Beckelman at Jackie's apartment door. There was some confusion as to why Beckelman was there, and he and Jackie had an exchange—in French—before she told him to let in the visitor.

"May I take your coat?" Jackie asked her.

"No, I'm fine, thank you," Beckelman said, suddenly too self-conscious to take off her coat in the bright-yellow entryway.

Jackie led her into the living room overlooking Central Park. Her apartment was furnished mostly with pieces from the family quarters at the White House, including some of the favorite things she inherited from two men she loved: a Louis XVI bureau on which Kennedy had signed the Nuclear Test Ban Treaty in 1963, and an ormolu-mounted Empire fall-front desk that was her father's. Billy Baldwin, her serial decorator, placed the pieces just so, arranging on the wall her drawings of animals and some small Indian paintings. Baldwin had covered Jackie's bedroom walls in ivory silk, and the bookshelves were lined with literature and Persian miniatures. Her bed was an extravagant gift from her longtime friend, the socialite Bunny Mellon. On the bed lay a rare guanaco fur spread that Jack had given her.[7] In the living room, Beckelman took note of John Jr.'s drum kit and the warmth of the space as she sat on the couch, handing Jackie the letter.

"Are you sure I can't take your coat?" Jackie implored.

"Oh, no thank you," stammered Beckelman, not one to typically be starstruck. She explained the reason for the letter, and the plans the Municipal Art Society had for a very public campaign to save the terminal. Jackie signed.

"My husband's ill," Jackie said matter-of-factly. "I'll be here. I want to get involved with something."

Beckelman was elated. She raced back to the MAS office.

"Kent," Beckelman gushed, "you've got to get her on the board. I had a great conversation with her. She's interested!"

If there was going to be a cause as part of Jackie's third act in life, the fight to save Grand Central had all of the elements that would appeal to her. Architectural enthusiasm and a love for the city of New York ran in Jackie's blood. Her maternal grandfather, James T. Lee, who had made a couple million dollars in real estate and banking in Manhattan before he was thirty, had won several awards for building designs, including 740 Park Avenue, which then, as now, was popular among the city's most elite.[8] New York was home, and Jackie embraced it, especially its architectural richness and history. Having spent summers at Hammersmith Farm in Newport, Rhode Island, where she and Jack were married, and having lived at Merrywood, her stepfather's Virginia estate, she respected old places and their craftsmanship. She had also traveled the world and seen the temples in Greece and Egypt, the ruins in Rome, Mexico, Ireland, and Cambodia, the Taj Mahal in India, and the mosques in Spain. She understood the enduring appeal of old buildings, what they said about the societies that created them, and how they became the very symbols of the places where they stood. Grand Central was no different. Who would come to Manhattan to see another office tower?

But most importantly, she understood the iconographic power of a building, the power of place, the feelings that could be evoked by the history of a facade, the precise tone of a paint color, a perfectly placed portrait, the scale of a room, or the balance of a public park. And there was one place more than any other that had drawn on all of her talents: 1600 Pennsylvania Avenue, her home for a thousand days.

Jackie first saw the White House when she was eleven on an Easter trip with her mother. "From the outside I remember the feeling of the place. But inside, all I can remember is shuffling through. There wasn't even a booklet you could buy," Jackie recalled.[9] Her impression did not improve when she returned as an official guest, when JFK was a senator and they attended receptions and lunches there together.

"The minute I knew that Jack was going to run for President I knew the White House would be one of my main projects if he won," she said.[10]

And it was.

"I'd read in the paper that it was customary for the First Lady to show the new one around," Jackie recalled in 1964. "And it was the last thing I wanted because, as I say, I was about to have this child. So I asked Tish [Baldrige, her Farmington friend whom she had chosen to be the new White House social secretary] to get in touch with Mary Jane McCaffrey, Mrs. Eisenhower's secretary. Mrs. Eisenhower told Mrs. McCaffrey not to give our people any help. But Tish knew her or somehow, so she used to meet Mary Jane, sneak away for lunch somewhere. And Tish liked Mary Jane very much, and she'd tell her, you know, things that you ought to know."[11]

Meanwhile, Jackie had also contacted Sister Parish, the decorator who had worked on the Kennedys' Georgetown house on N Street, as well as their Hyannis Port residence and their soon-to-be rental, Glen Ora, a country estate in Middleburg, Virginia.

"Can you help me with the 'house with the columns'?" Jackie playfully wrote Parish. She even wondered if Parish would pose as her aunt for the walk-through with Eisenhower.

"First of all," Parish responded to Jackie, "I think I must tell you that for your sake I think it would be wrong for me to be your aunt. I am so afraid you might get into trouble. I assume they take names, etc. and probably go so far as checking. I may be wrong." [12]

Instead of visiting, Parish obtained some miniature blueprints at the New York Public Library. "And it was from these tiny documents that I did my initial thinking and planning about the White House, the interiors of which I had never seen," Parish said. "I had very little to go on except my knowledge of the President and Mrs. Kennedy's taste and the additional request from her that I try to duplicate as closely as possible the feeling of the rooms in the [Kennedy] house on N Street." [13]

Mamie Eisenhower initially refused to see Jackie, exclaiming, "This is my house, and nobody's going to see it!" [14] But the press pushed her to invite Jackie for a tour, a private walkthrough on December 9, 1960, at noon, the same day Jackie was being released from Georgetown Hospital with baby John and just a few hours before the Kennedys were due to leave for Palm Beach.

"Like a fool," Jackie recalled, "I said I'd go." [15]

Mrs. Eisenhower instructed White House usher J. B. West to "please have the rooms in order, but no servants on the upstairs floors. And I plan to leave [the White House] at 1:30, so have my car ready." [16]

West told Eisenhower that he had already received a call from Jackie's secret service agent, requesting a wheelchair be there for the incoming First Lady when she arrived for the tour.

"Oh, dear. I wanted to take her around alone," Eisenhower frowned, drumming her fingers on the nightstand. The truth was the grand woman did not want to push around a political enemy. "I'll tell you what. We'll get a wheelchair, but put it behind a door somewhere, out of sight. It will be available *if she asks for it.*"[17]

President-elect Kennedy wheeled Jackie and their newborn out of the hospital through a throng of reporters and photographers to a waiting white sedan, where a Massachusetts nurse who had worked with sixteen of Rose Kennedy's seventeen grandchildren held the baby swaddled tightly in the backseat next to Jackie. They went home, where Jackie changed out of her black-and-white checked suit and red beret, put on a black dress, three-strand pearls, a purple coat, black gloves, a small black fur hat, and slipped out the back to avoid reporters.[18] A secret service agent drove her, in the front seat next to him, straight for a private tour of the White House, which was decorated for Christmas. When they pulled up the circular drive of the south portico, a doorman helped her out of the car.

Jackie was thin and pale, but as West approached to introduce himself he noticed that she also appeared shockingly young, thirty years younger than any First Lady he had served.

"I'm Mr. West, the Chief Usher," he said.

"I'm Jacqueline Kennedy," she whispered.

She walked hesitantly through the Diplomatic Reception Room, taking in all the furnishings—the rugs, the walls—and continued to the elevator.

"Mrs. Eisenhower is waiting upstairs," he said.

They took the elevator to the second floor and Jackie took a deep breath as Mamie Eisenhower came into sight in the hall.

"Hello, Mrs. Kennedy," the First Lady said, extending her hand. "I do hope you are feeling much better now. And how is the baby?"

With the wheelchair hidden in a closet by the elevator, West excused himself. Jackie walked slowly—and painfully— around the White House. Eisenhower showed her all the floors and rooms, referring to it as "my house" and "my carpets" and never offered to have her sit.[19] The decor was revoltingly institutional. There were water fountains sticking out of the walls— and Jackie knew she had to do something to fix it. She had good reason to want to properly renovate and preserve the White House. Not only did she have to live there (and its disheveled state was below her standards), but it was also symbolically the nation's home. Furthermore, the Kennedy White House would mark a turning point in the political use of television to communicate with the public, and Jackie knew that 1600 Pennsylvania Avenue would be the president's stage. It needed to inspire.

The White House had been burned, doused, trashed, picked apart, and callously revamped. Abigail Adams hung her wash in the East Room. James Madison, presiding over the War of 1812, was forced to flee with his wife, Dolley, in 1814 when the

British stormed the building, ate the president's meal, and then lit the place on fire, reducing it to a blackened sandstone shell before rain eventually drenched the flames. Within three years James Monroe—who had been minister to France—reopened the White House with $500,000 in restoration funds from Congress, sneaking in the European pieces to avoid any "buy American" political backlash. There was more: Andrew Jackson's wild farewell reception had overwhelmed the building; Civil War soldiers, dressed in soiled uniforms, had snipped swatches from the draperies as souvenirs; and the bad design taste of more than a few presidents had left its mark. In 1881, President Chester Arthur, a widower, auctioned twenty-four wagonloads of old furniture and hired Louis Tiffany to dress the mansion in lavish Victorian fashion. In 1902, Theodore Roosevelt hired architect Stanford White to undo the damage. But then, in the 1920s, despite his reputation for being a proponent of smaller government, Calvin Coolidge added eighteen rooms to the third floor, damaging the structural integrity of the place. The White House had become so run-down that Harry Truman gutted the mansion in 1948 and put it back together, adding a balcony—to much criticism—off the third-floor private quarters, dispensing bits of the old place (like a marble mantelpiece) to his political cronies, and filling it with reproduction furniture from B. Altman.[20]

The Eisenhowers, who lived in the White House next and for two terms, hadn't helped much. Mamie liked pink.

The "house had been run like a military camp the past

sixteen years or so and lacks female taste,"[21] Baldrige reported to Jackie after her own visit with Eisenhower's staff.

Not only did the Eisenhowers typically eat their dinner on trays in front of the television but the furnishings were also a haphazard collection of leftovers that reflected the different tastes of every four- or eight-year occupation—as well as the surprisingly different economic, geographic, and social backgrounds that the presidents until then had come from.

Exactly an hour and ten minutes after Jackie's White House tour with Mamie Eisenhower had begun, the usher was buzzed, signaling the end.

The two women walked out of the mansion together, shook hands, posed for a picture, and said a Spartan good-bye. Mrs. Eisenhower, wearing a gray broadtail coat and black satin pillbox hat, stepped into the backseat of her Chrysler limousine, on her way to play cards. Jackie lowered herself gently into her three-year-old station wagon. West approached the car to hand blueprints to Jackie, but the pain was evident on her face. Jackie had not seen the wheelchair and so never requested it.[22]

"Could you please send them to Palm Beach for me?" she asked, referring to the documents. "We're going to rest there until Inauguration Day."

Jackie headed to the Kennedy family's waterfront retreat in Florida later that day. She was on the verge of exhaustion and most likely postpartum depression.

"I couldn't stop crying for about two days," Jackie recalled. "It was something that takes away your last strength when you don't have any left. So that wasn't very nice of Mrs. Eisenhower."[23]

Although Jackie was a veteran consumer of interior design services, renovating a typical home—even large and luxurious ones like those to which she had been accustomed—paled in comparison to the overwhelming task of restoring the White House. And, to top it off, she was recovering from the cesarean and worried about John Jr., who was born prematurely. Her husband was about to become president, and she had to move. For most women, any one of those issues would have been enough to cause panic. Jackie had to deal with all of it, and look gorgeous in the process. Despite feeling overwhelmed by the job that she was thrusting on herself, Jackie met the challenge in a way that was both familiar and comforting, by delving both into books and the archival material that West had given her, including a collection of pictures of all the various rooms and what they were like at the time. In Palm Beach, Jackie wrote down what she wanted done and sent it to the decorator. She began firing off memos to West while Sister Parish sent her samples.[24]

The Palm Beach house, an old home that Joe Kennedy had bought about thirty years before, had no air-conditioning and was overpopulated with all of his children, in-laws, and grandkids, hardly a place to rest and recuperate. In addition to the White House project, Oleg Cassini was designing Jackie's wardrobe and needed her approval on sketches that conveyed a philosophical "look," not just pretty dresses. Jack was choosing his cabinet. John Jr. was not thriving and required special care from a local pediatrician who "really saved his life," Jackie said later. "I was ill and recuperating in the room I shared with dear Jack. The house was so crowded. He was writing his inaugural speech in the room, I remember the yellow [note] pages being strewn all around the room. And when he left I would get up and try to keep them together under some weight on the desk. Someone would come in the room and have conferences with Jack. So I would go sit in the bathroom till it was over. I didn't come to meals, I couldn't hold any food down." [25]

Jackie stayed in her room, even rebuffing requests from her mother-in-law to take meals with important guests.

Adding to her stress during what was supposed to be a time of recuperation, a would-be assassin who thought Kennedy had bought the election was carrying seven sticks of dynamite that he planned to detonate as he drove his car into Kennedy's one Sunday at church. But when the attacker saw the couple emerge on North Ocean Boulevard, the sight of Jackie gave him second thoughts. "I did not wish to harm her or the children," the man, Richard Pavlick, told the Secret Service. "I decided to get him at the church or some place later." [26] His plot was foiled before he could act.

The night after the inauguration, when Jack and Jackie settled in to the private quarters of the White House, they were seated in regal, tall-backed "host" and "hostess" chairs in a formal dining room. They hated the seating, and much of what else they saw. The chairs promptly went into storage, along with a mirrored screen and a silver replica of a ship.[27] Their new home reeked of paint fumes. But they couldn't open the windows because they were stuck shut, having not been open for years.

On their second day in the White House, Jackie focused on the children's rooms, huddling with Sister Parish and Joseph Karitas, the White House painter, in Caroline's room, where Jackie instructed him to paint a mahogany bureau off-white, "not too yellow, and she wanted glaze. Then she wanted gold stripes and then she wanted some pink stripes, light pink, to set it off. So she would draw a little plan," Karitas remembered. He would frequently receive these sketches from her and could see that she was the type who would change her mind about colors and styles. Painting a dresser was child's play compared with the tasks before him, which included repainting of trim, refinishing of floors, and applications of special glazes to make walls look old.[28]

It is clear that not only was Jackie's taste particular and refined but she also channeled a great deal of her creative energy into an endeavor that seemed suitable for a bored, midcentury housewife, especially one with means—decorating. "I remember when she got that N Street house, it was going to be just right—it was going to be absolutely marvelous," Jackie's mother recalled of the other Kennedy Georgetown house that Sister Parish had worked on. "It was a house with a lot of feeling about it and a lot of charm, but she did that living room, the double living room downstairs, over at least three times within the first four months they were there. I remember you could go there one day and there would be two beautiful needlepoint rugs, one in the little front drawing room and one in the back one towards the garden. The next week they would both be gone. They would have been sent on trial. Not only that, but the curtains were apt to be red chintz one week . . ."[29]

Changing the decor of a townhouse is one thing, but tinkering with the White House, quite another. Two weeks after the inauguration, Jackie and the president had lunch with their trusted adviser and personal friend Clark Clifford, who cautioned Jackie about a lack of funds and how the White House was a "sacred cow," not to be toyed with. "Woe to any president that changes it," he told them.

Clifford suggested a fine arts committee to provide some political cover, drew up the legal framework for it, and by February 23, 1961, the group was empowered to "locate authentic furniture of the date of the building of the White House and the raising of funds to purchase this furniture as gifts for the White House."[30] While the committee was mostly stocked with amateur antiques "experts," they were wealthy and had good networks that would be important for success.

One of Jackie's friends recommended the eighty-one-year-old Republican millionaire and antiques expert Henry du Pont, founder of the Winterthur Museum in Delaware, as chairman of the committee. He accepted. "It was the biggest red-letter day of all," Jackie said of his appointment to the fourteen-member committee.

With the committee in place, Jackie realized she also needed a decorator who would be able to find and arrange the pieces needed to reflect James Monroe's French Empire style. Parish was known for her "undecorated look" that suited small casual rooms. This was the White House, and it required a much grander approach. So she added to the team Stéphane Boudin of Jansen in Paris, who had renovated part of Versailles and had agreed to do the White House work for free.[31] Not surprisingly, his arrival created friction and chaos. Boudin insisted Parish cancel some of her orders so he could take a room in a new direction. He clashed with Du Pont, whose stiff East Coast temperament was at odds with the "dramatic little Frenchman," as West called him. But Jackie gradually favored Boudin over Parish for a few reasons, confiding that she "learned more about architecture from Boudin than from all the books I could have read."[32] There was also a rumor going around that Parish had kicked Caroline.[33] Even if true, Jackie was also upset because she felt Parish had overcharged her for redecorating her rented Glen Ora weekend home in Virginia, the bills for which were sent to the office of her father-in-law, Joseph P. Kennedy, in New York, where all family financial matters were handled. The exorbitant charges for some accessories embarrassed Jackie—or at least she pretended they did—because her father-in-law would have to pay for it, as this memo from a Kennedy family office employee to Parish implies:

*Dear Mrs. Parish . . . Mrs. Kennedy was horrified to see that
she was being charged fifty dollars a piece for two waste baskets
and thirty-five dollars a piece for two tissue boxes. She never
requested hand-painted designs to be applied to these; what she
asked for were ordinary department store scrap baskets and
Kleenex boxes to be covered with wallpaper used in the room,
as she had done here in Washington, at Miriam Crocker's, before
for approximately $7.50 for the waste basket and $5.00 for
the tissue box. Mrs. Kennedy would like to know if you could
do the same for the same amounts as Miriam Crocker, taking the
present ones back.*[34]

It may seem that such things would have been beneath her watch, especially given the enormity of the White House job. But they weren't. West regularly received handwritten lists of instructions that Jackie would jot on her yellow legal pad. West called her "the ideas girl." She directed fabric orders, requested the story behind a certain antique, set standards for how flowers were arranged, and decided what tables should be used at state dinners (small round ones rather than one large U-shaped table).[35] She personally designed ashtray stands, as well as paperweights for official gifts from the president to other dignitaries.[36] She was studious and intense about the project, and clearly someone who appreciated history. To complete the Treaty Room, she fired off a memo to West telling him that original documents should be framed and organized to complement their significance:

I was looking at treaties—in Treaty Room. a.) They should all be ones that were signed in that room. That would be [Andrew] Johnson—TR—isn't that right? Or did J Q Adams use that as office and sign treaties there—? Is there any way of finding out which were signed in office—when [sic] room was that—and which when it was Cabinet Room—probably not. So I think—as Treaty of Peace with Spain is obviously in that room—we should just have Johnson—TR—and lots more. Let's get rid of FDR and Cuba—and get lots more treaties of 1864–1902. We could put them way up [on] walls. b.) Where the name of treaty is printed on mat—I think date should be printed also—as it is too complicated to read treaty to find out.[37]

Despite her annoyances with Parish, she needed to keep the American on the decorating team for political cover. She also knew she needed to hire a "real" curator, and she did—the first one the White House ever had. She was Lorraine Waxman Pearce, a twenty-six-year-old mother who was both an oddity and a media sensation as a working woman at a time when being such was still rare. Pearce was an expert in French influences on American decorative arts of the early nineteenth century, and had been working at the Winterthur Museum. It would be Pearce's job to help bring back American furnishings and artwork that mirrored the periods or presidential namesakes of various rooms.

With the inventory not yet complete and the committee in place, Jackie put out a public call to anyone who had a chair, a desk, a vase—anything at all from the White House that they would be willing to donate. In doing so, she cast a spell on the country and sent families digging through their attics for something with provenance. Her request produced an avalanche of mail from people saying they had something of "importance" to give back.[38]

On her first day on the job in March 1961, Pearce was ushered into a room that was knee-high with stacks of public mail where people had responded to the announcement. "I've got a chair"; "I've got my grandmother's stays"; "I've got an old toothbrush that belonged to General Grant," the letters said.[39]

To create something out of chaos, Pearce, with no staff, began cataloging White House furnishings, their history, and their possible location throughout the world. After Abraham Lincoln's assassination, his destitute wife had sold much of their furniture and locating those pieces was a big part of the restoration effort. And there were many successes. Treasury Secretary Douglas Dillon donated a room full of American Empire furniture that included a Dolley Madison sofa. An original Monroe chair was donated by a woman from Pennsylvania. And Sister Parish gave one of her own Victorian settees and two side chairs that had belonged to the Lincolns. There also was a Hepplewhite mirror, with golden eagle decoration, that had once hung in a tavern where Washington bade farewell to his generals.

Meanwhile, it was the committee's job to go through the

White House room by room, assess its contents, and decide what pieces needed to be acquired to properly complete it. It was an exhaustive process, with Jackie immersed in it.

One undated memo, written by Jackie and Du Pont, found that the Family Dining Room needed an overhaul.

Comments on the room at the present time:
The chairs in English Chippendale style are not appropriate.
The Adam commode against the south wall is too early in style.
The sideboard and cabinet, while suitable in style, are not antique.
The rug seems appropriate in size and in the scale of its pattern; the
*   color is quite agreeable.*

Suggested Changes:
The room should be furnished with American Hepplewhite or
*   Sheraton pieces.*
The curtains should be hung within the window moldings.
The chairs and commode should be replaced.
The sideboard and cabinet can be kept here until better pieces are
*   found.*

Furniture Needed:
Eight chairs
One sideboard
One cabinet
One commode or semicircular chest of drawers
One screen [40]

And that was just one little room.

Despite being exhausted from the work, from parenting, from the relentless stress that she and her husband faced every day, Jackie was determined to make the White House a more memorable place than the one she had seen when she was eleven.

She scoured old receipts and photographs to find objects, their origins, and where they belonged in the White House, snagging four Cézanne paintings originally intended for the White House but hanging in the National Gallery of Art. She hung those in the family quarters and moved a Grandma Moses painting of the Fourth of July into Caroline's room.[41] She toured the mansion with those who knew it firsthand—FDR Jr. and Truman. She consulted historians and made spelunking expeditions with Pearce to the basement, plucking out furniture for the fifty-four rooms and sixteen bathrooms. Jackie and Pearce snarled their stockings, got their hands dirty, and found unexpected treasures, including Teddy Roosevelt's rugs, Monroe's gold and silver French flatware and—most important of all—a heavy oak desk that was piled with electronics in the broadcast room. A carved inscription revealed that Queen Victoria had given it to President Hayes; it was built of old timbers from the HMS *Resolute*, a British ship that had sailed to the Arctic in 1852, gotten trapped in ice, abandoned, and was later recovered by a Yankee whaler. The ship was refitted in the United States and sent back to Britain as a gift. The Queen returned the sentiment, sending it back as a desk. Jackie had it set up in the Oval office. John Jr. loved to crawl beneath it.

Ever resourceful, Jackie didn't waste her time with underlings. She went straight to the source to get what she wanted, including a painting of Benjamin Franklin for the White House, but only two existed. She wrote a gushing letter to Walter Annenberg, who owned one of them, saying, "Mr. Annenberg you are the leading citizen of Philadelphia and that's why I'm turning to you—because we need in the White House a portrait of the man who in his day was the leading citizen of Philadelphia, Benjamin Franklin. Don't you think that a great Philadelphia citizen should give the White House a portrait of a great Philadelphia citizen?" Annenberg, after thinking it over, donated the portrait, which had cost him $250,000.[42] The response to her letter helped Jackie understand the power of her pen.

On another occasion, she called Bernard Boutin, a former Kennedy campaign worker and mayor of Laconia, New Hampshire, who was rewarded with the title of administrator of the General Services Administration, a man whose alliance would be needed for an even greater purpose, of which neither was yet aware. Were there any busts in the archives of Presidents Jackson, Roosevelt, and Jefferson to place in the little niches above the doorways in the cabinet room? When none could be found, she had replicas made.[43]

She was a demanding boss, sending endless memos to staff, such as this one to Sister Parish:

I can see our big need is a sofa table—4 good ones are all in Jack's bedroom now—something with XVI galley or finials like in my Va bedroom—I think I should buy—If you have to have them made I can see picture first.

    XO

    J.[44]

The job also required reams of fabric, which meant there was a constant hunt for the finest materials and kept one man in particular, White House upholsterer Lawrence J. Arata, busy for a long time. Although the job was supposed to last only for six weeks, it became full-time—and he was so busy that he was married on a Wednesday and returned to work the next day, with the First Lady saying she "felt very sorry that we couldn't have more time off." [45]

By summer, Jackie was honing in on serious donors, employing more disarming handwritten letters on distinctive White House stationery. Using a mix of charm, flattery, and down-to-earth style, the length of Jackie's letters grew with the enormity of what she was asking for. To one couple, Mr. and Mrs. Loeb, she wrote a long note that went on for eleven paragraphs and included a detailed wish list that ended with: "P.S. Forgive this endless letter—I think I must get larger writing paper!" [46]

As with the letter to Annenberg, this letter moved the Loebs to provide her with a pair of $3,500 chenets, a pair of $6,500 appliqués, a suite of Louis XVI furniture (canapé, six open arm chairs, four side chairs, and the restoration for all, totaling nearly $25,000; a $5,200 bench; and a mantel with repair, packing, and shipping that came to $1,273.20). In addition to the $38,780 tab, the Loebs were considering another $72,000 in contributions, including a $20,000 chandelier.[47]

Her curatorial approach, not surprisingly, extended to the White House library, which was filled with Agatha Christie mysteries and contemporary books that publishers sent to the White House. "Books that are presented to JFK and me I want for our own library—so send to me," she wrote in an undated memo. "The library will be stocked by a committee—It will include all Presidential writings + books that have influenced American thought—so we don't want to clutter it up with what are our souvenirs. 2) on All state visits—abroad + here—have JFK give a set of his books—I) *Eng* 2) *Profiles* 3) *Strategy* 4) *Tide* *—inscribed + signed—That is what Nehru did for us—+ it is a great present and makes up for what we can't spend."[48]

Jackie put Arthur Schlesinger Jr., the historian and special assistant to the president, in charge of the selection of books for the library.[49] And it was the job of Yale's librarian, James T. Babb, to execute the project, forming a committee to solicit donations, hunt for, and vet important first editions.[50]

By September, nine months into the job, Jackie had convinced Congress to pass legislation that would allow furniture of "historic or artistic interest" to become the property of the White House, with the Smithsonian Institution to hold[51] on loan any object not on display or in use. The Ground Floor Corridor and the principle public rooms of the first floor would

---

* The books were: *Why England Slept, Profiles in Courage, The Strategy of Peace,* and *To Turn the Tide.*

July 1961. Jackie examines a set of blueprints as White House curator Lorraine Pearce talks on the phone, Washington, DC. *(Ed Clark/Time Life Pictures/Getty Images)*

be recognized as worthy of primary attention and their museum character.

She was also ready to reveal glimpses of the work to the American people, and had learned from the experts—the Kennedys themselves—how to use the media to build support for an idea. She handpicked reporter Hugh Sidey, whose campaign coverage in *Time* had always been favorable, to interview her about her White House efforts.

"I had a backache every day for three months," Jackie told Sidey, who was scribbling in his notebook.[52] "Like any President's wife I'm here for only a brief time," she said, eerily foreshadowing Camelot's one thousand days. "And before everything slips away, before every link with the past is gone, I want to do this."

But renovating the White House was more than a patriotic calling. It was an outlet for a very smart woman. She once told a reporter during the 1960 presidential campaign while giving a tour of their Georgetown home, "I love my house! It is my expression of myself."[53]

In addition to the White House interview with Sidey, she agreed to tape a special tour for television. On Valentine's Day 1962, all of America—or at least those with TVs—would be treated to a one-hour broadcast of Jackie explaining her White House work. The Kennedys were no different than everyone else eagerly awaiting the start of the show at 10:00 PM. They had invited some people over to join them for the viewing, with drinks and dinner at the White House before it aired, including

Benjamin C. Bradlee, then of *Newsweek*, and his wife, Tony. Despite the fact it was Valentine's Day and he was in the company of friends, the president was in a foul mood.

"My wife went so far as to say later that she felt the president was actually jealous of Jackie's performance and the attention she got as a result," Bradlee wrote in his diary later that night.[54]

The group gathered around a TV near the Lincoln Room to watch the show on NBC, which had been taped a month earlier during a session that took nearly eight hours, at a production cost of more than $250,000.[55] They were rapt and in virtual silence as they watched Jackie, in a dark two-piece wool bouclé day dress by Rodier, whose red color was lost on the black-and-white program.[56]

The televised tour began in the curator's office on the ground floor and moved to the Diplomatic Reception Room. The camera took in the original kitchen, which FDR had used as a broadcast room, and showed how the space had become an upholstery shop as well as an office space where Jackie and Pearce were producing a 132-page guidebook—something Jackie had wanted since her very first visit to the White House—and that they had been working on for a year. (She had to lobby the president to get him to agree to it because his staff was complaining it would be "an outrage" and a desecration to do something so commercial.)[57] Then they went on to the East Room, where balls take place, the State Dining Room, which was set with a gold-and-white tablecloth and china, as well as the Red, Blue, and Green rooms—all difficult to grasp without Technicolor. The show skipped over the Library because it was not yet ready.[58]

Jackie explained in a soft voice from the TV what the history, the relevance, and the reasoning was behind the placement of various pieces in the White House, while thanking those who gifted them as part of the permanent collection.

Near the end of the show, the president briefly joined his wife on-camera in the Monroe Room, which was then still in the process of being renovated as the president's cabinet room. The president extolled Jackie's work, explained why it was so important that the White House reflect the living history of the republic, and then said two memorable things on-camera. First, he said, "Past is prologue." Second, the president said that maybe some of the White House visitors would be inspired to return as residents. "Even the girls."

The camera panned to Jackie, who would win an Emmy for her work. She blinked and showed no expression.[59]

While 50 million viewers went to bed that night marveling at the White House renovation (millions more would see it in the UK on BBC), far fewer were aware of the other major preservation story playing out that same day at Washington's Lafayette Square, in which Jackie was also embroiled.

Lafayette Square was a quadrangle of intimate nineteenth-century Federalist-style townhomes around a green where diplomats, publishers, cabinet members, and other American notables such as Dolley Madison and Daniel Webster had lived. The square was quite literally the traditional front yard of the White House until Pennsylvania Avenue cut between them. Pierre L'Enfant, who had designed the Capitol after being appointed by George Washington, referred to the square in his plans as the "President's Park." [60]

By 1957, with the federal government expanding and the square falling into disrepair, President Eisenhower had targeted many of the buildings around Lafayette Square for demolition. Initially, Eisenhower wanted to replace the homes with a modernist executive office building that would occupy an entire block. Those who lived and worked in the targeted buildings complained.[61] Then-senator John F. Kennedy initially fought on their behalf. But the government's plan, backed by Congress, plodded along.

In his first week as president, Kennedy enlisted an old friend, Bill Walton, to help him find a solution for Lafayette Square. Walton was an artist and former war correspondent for *Time-Life* and was a longtime pal of JFK's, a frequent Hyannis Port houseguest, and after the inauguration his friendship and loyalty had been rewarded with insider status.

Walton did not like the Eisenhower plans and showed them to Jackie. "They're wildly unattractive plans for modern government," he said. She agreed it was not the kind of architecture she wanted facing the White House.

"Until the bulldozers move, we're ahead and you can't give up," she told Walton, who knew she meant it.[62]

The papers began calling Walton the czar of Lafayette Square. But he struggled to find an alternative that made everyone happy. Like most things in Washington, politics was interfering. Congress was applying pressure and requiring that the new space have a certain amount of square footage, which could not be built, according to the assessment of two Boston architectural firms, if the homes facing the square were saved.

Walton was buckling. He told the president that the Dolley Madison house, built in 1820 and a place where Mrs. Madison held social teas in her post–White House years, had been completely changed when it was remodeled as the Cosmos Club in 1895 and had lost its historical significance; it was then serving as government offices. He said the Tayloe House and the Belasco Theatre had also been stripped of their importance, leaving only one building—the Decatur House, built in 1818—worth saving.

To the alarm of preservationists—including his own wife—the president took Walton's advice and approved some of the plans. Jackie was furious with Walton and her husband, who clearly had larger issues to deal with, including Khrushchev, de Gaulle, and nuclear weapons testing.

But newspapers were reporting that the president was caving on Lafayette Square.

"President Kennedy had briefly raised the traditionalists' hopes that a last-minute rescue would save the [Lafayette] Square's town-green atmosphere from the wrecker's ball and functional Federal architecture. Despite shots still being fired by lovers of the status quo, the president is not expected to halt the razing of most of the old houses and buildings on the east and west sides of the square," the *New York Times* reported on the day Jackie's White House tour aired.[63] (The story was another likely reason for JFK's discontent that night.)

Jackie went to work as a preservationist once again—the very next day. On February 15, 1962, she asked David Finley, then chairman of the US Commission of Fine Arts, to take a walk around Lafayette Square with her [64] and understand why the proposed buildings were out of line.

"In France," she told him, with the White House in the backdrop, "there is a law providing that certain buildings of historical or architectural importance could not be destroyed. It would be nice for Congress to have such a law.

"Mr. Finley," she urged, "these building can be preserved. And they must."

Finley told her that the president and the US Commission of Fine Arts had already signed off on the plans, but that the final decision would be made by Boutin at the General Services Administration, the independent agency that oversees the basic functioning of federal agencies, such as procurement and cost minimizing. After her walk with Finley, she reached out to Boutin right away, who told her the contracts had already been signed.

But Boutin heard her intense desire to stop the plan and told her he'd prevent any further money to be spent until they had a strategy in place.

"I'll slow it right down to a walk," he told her.

Although she was busy getting ready for what would be her iconic trip to India and Pakistan with her sister the next week, Jackie followed up her conversation with an impassioned letter to Boutin, again employing flattery and charm. "Unfortunately, last summer the president okayed some plans for buildings; he was in a hurry, he doesn't have time to bother himself with details like this, he trusted the advice of a friend . . . and I really don't think it was the right advice," she wrote. "With all he has to do, at least I can spare him some minor problems like this. So I turn to you for help . . . All architects are innovators and would rather do something totally new than in the spirit of old buildings. I think they are totally wrong in this case, as the important thing is to preserve the 19th-century feeling of Lafayette Square . . . Write to the architects and tell them to submit a design that is more in keeping with the 19th-century bank on the corner. It should be the same color, same size, etc." [65]

Boutin was impressed that "she could see right off quick that the previous architect had a vested interest in having the new buildings developed."

While Jackie and Lee were in India in March 1962, riding on elephants, meeting with Prime Minister Nehru and his daughter, Indira Gandhi, and visiting the Taj Mahal and other historic sites, the president knew that when she came back, she would be more—not less—convinced of her position on Lafayette Square. He needed a plan. By sheer coincidence, architect Jack Warnecke was in Washington and called his Stanford fraternity brother Red Fay (then undersecretary of the navy), who invited him to a reception in the Oval Office the next day. Kennedy had met Warnecke in California and heard about his playing left tackle on the undefeated Stanford football team, which lead to Kennedy's nickname for him.

"Rosebowl! What the hell are you doing here?" the president asked Warnecke when he spotted the San Franciscan in the Oval Office. The two talked briefly—the president was distracted by several lovely women in attendance—and then the next day Kennedy asked Fay what Warnecke did for a living.

"He's a very successful architect," Fay said.

"Have him call me tomorrow morning at nine-thirty. Jackie is very upset about the plans for the new building to be put up on Lafayette Square. She feels that what they are planning will ruin the beauty and historic charm of this area, and I agree with her." [66]

After the debriefing, Warnecke was told to call Walton with a new scheme.

On the surface, Warnecke would have seemed an unlikely savior. He had been trained by Walter Gropius, the godfather of modernism—the movement that was at the root of all this tearing down—at Harvard's Graduate School of Design, where Breuer had taught. But much of what Gropius and other modernists such as Le Corbusier had stood for was being challenged by a New York housewife named Jane Jacobs, who in 1961 published a seminal book called *The Death and Life of Great American Cities*. The book criticized modernist planning policies that she claimed were destroying many urban enclaves. Jackie, a voracious reader, had most likely read the influential book. Warnecke, meanwhile, had developed a reputation for contextual architecture, blending the old and the new in ways that were both comfortable and exciting—precisely what he designed for Lafayette Square. His plan, approved by Jackie, allowed for the construction of an office building and a courthouse—set back from the street, without taking a wrecking ball to most of the square. Essentially the buildings would be constructed behind the old facades. Furthermore, the Madison house would be restored by removing exterior stucco.

"Underneath is the original brick, in as good shape as that on Decatur House across the square," Warnecke reported.[67]

Jackie won. Many of the historic facades would remain, and the new development would be set back in a less noticeable way.

A few weeks after that walk through the square, Finley decided to step down as chairman of the Fine Arts Commission and Jackie wrote an impassioned twelve-page handwritten letter full of exclamation points on White House stationery to Walton, urging him to become Finley's successor or else "lovely buildings will be torn down—+ cheesy skyscrapers go up— Perhaps saving old buildings + having the new ones be right isn't the most important thing in the world—if you are waiting for the bomb—but I think we are always going to be waiting for the bomb + it won't ever come + so to save the old—+ to make the new beautiful is terribly important— and the real estate operators are your enemy."[68]

Jackie reviewing plans for Lafayette Square with architect John Warnecke (left) and GSA administrator Bernard Boutin. She is wearing the same Chanel suit that she wore on the day of the assassination. *(Courtesy of JFK Library)*

Jackie's success fed her desire to do more about the square. Boutin noticed that "the refurbishment of the White House really got her started and then she never took another breath, she just kept going." Rarely a day went by when he did not at least get a call from her wanting to know how the new plans for Lafayette Square were progressing. He would take new drawings to the White House and go over them with her, laying out the drawings on the floor and reviewing them on hands and knees.

By October 1962, the plans had progressed enough such that Jackie was ready to unveil them to the media. And she orchestrated that event, too. As her car pulled up to the GSA building for the press conference, Boutin was waiting. In a check skirt suit with her hair swept up in a beehive with bangs, Jackie walked into the auditorium saying repeatedly to him, "Bernie, remember, not *me*, the *president*."

Whether it was false modesty or she was truly being the ever-political wife, Jackie wanted to be on the record that her husband should receive all of the credit for the win. But the mere fact that she had to remind Boutin to do so was an admission that she had been the driving force, the will to get it done at a time when the president couldn't because, as the most powerful man in the world, how could he micromanage his front yard?

Also, despite the fact that she never answered any questions during the event—except when one reporter asked off topic about the crabgrass on the White House lawn—her mere presence at the press conference ensured that she would be photographed inspecting the architectural model of two new large buildings set behind the historic facades. And that would get people to pay attention in a way they might not even if her husband were in the photo.

"I believe that the importance of Lafayette Square lies in the fact that we were not willing to destroy our cultural and historic heritage," Boutin announced, reading from the president's letter, "but that we were willing to find means of preserving it while still meeting the requirements of growth in government."[69]

This is not to say all would be saved. The old Belasco Theatre on Madison Place would make room for an arched entryway to the new US Court of Claims and the US Court of Customs and Patent Appeals. And the buildings that once served as the headquarters for the National Grange and the Brookings Institution would meet the wrecking ball.

As First Lady, restoring the White House and saving Lafayette Square were not the only preservation issues that would prepare Jackie for the Grand Central battle. The other was quite personal and involved the future of her girlhood home: Merrywood. Her mother and stepfather were contemplating the unthinkable—selling the place to a developer who would build apartment towers on the site overlooking the Potomac.

Hughdie and Janet Auchincloss had a hard choice to make. Sell Merrywood, the McLean, Virginia, estate where they had been spending winters since their wedding in 1942, or continue to let the property drain them financially. The place was huge, a two-story Georgian mansion, with thirteen bedrooms, ten bathrooms, a four-car garage with another five bedrooms above that, a tenant house, and a five-room gardener's cottage.[70] Despite its size, Jackie and her family no longer spent time there. Jack was president and Jackie was busy sketching the layout of a country estate they would build on a mountaintop in nearby Atoka, Virginia; they would call it Wexford, after the county in Ireland where Kennedy's ancestors came from, but the couple only used it twice before the assassination.[71]

A month before Jackie's televised White House tour, Hughdie had sold an option on the Merrywood property to a local developer who wanted to build three brick luxury apartment towers as tall as seventeen stories—some higher than the Capitol—and two rows of townhouses on the Merrywood

Merrywood in MacLean, Virginia, during the Auchincloss family's ownership. *(Origin unknown)*

property, which was just down the road from the recently built CIA headquarters in Langley. The residence was to be turned into a private club and guesthouse. In order to move forward, the project, which could house as many as twelve hundred families and cost about $15 million, needed Fairfax County to approve a zoning change.

The residents of the powerful, leafy suburb—a wealthy bedroom community for spies, diplomats, and, of course, members of the Kennedy administration—were educated, motivated, and privileged. They had been voting for local officials who were against development and had been fighting apartments for some time when the Merrywood issue erupted. Almost immediately, citizens' groups began drawing the sharp contrast between Jackie's preservation efforts and what her mother and stepfather were threatening to do, highlighting the "incongruity" of the situation.[72]

Jackie was in a horrible bind. She loved Merrywood so much that she wrote home about it to her stepfather from Italy when she was younger: "I began to feel terribly homesick as I was driving—just like a dream—I started thinking of things like the path leading to the stable at Merrywood with the stones slipping as you ran up it." Jack was fond of the place, too. The couple had spent their first summer as husband and wife on the property. Hughdie and Janet didn't need so much space. But they did need the money the development deal would bring, not fully appreciating the political problems it would cause the Kennedys.

In late April 1962, the county, by a 5 to 2 vote, approved the necessary zoning change to turn Merrywood into an apartment complex, prompting a mass protest at a local school. Auchincloss, meanwhile, was coming under heavy fire from the media about his plans to push forward. The fight had many of the hallmarks of a local zoning battle, but the intrigue of a much bigger story involving Jackie, Bobby Kennedy—whose house at Hickory Hill also was in McLean—and the president himself.[73] Despite the legal drama, the developer vowed to exercise his option to build.[74] And he did.

Then Associate Supreme Court Justice William O. Douglas got in the act, calling the proposed apartments "destructive of the [Potomac] river's shoreline beauty." And the Federal Aviation Agency administrator asserted that pilots approaching National Airport would object to the buildings' height. Auchincloss was asked to cancel the sale, but he declined. "I've got to stick to my contract. I think it's a good thing for the county to have . . . It will bring a lot more money into the county, which they need badly. The apartment buildings didn't appeal much to my aesthetic but that's their (the developers') business." As for the protesters, he said, "I think they are setting a bad example."[75]

While just about everyone she knew was being sucked into the Merrywood vortex, Jackie was studiously avoiding the situation, at least publicly.[76] But it is clear where the Kennedy administration stood.

By November 16, 1963, a week before Kennedy's assassination, the developer had begun clearing the land when the

US Department of the Interior made an unprecedented move. Instead of negotiating, it went straight to court to block construction, eventually paying $744,000 for scenic rights. Interior Secretary Stewart Udall, an early environmentalist who also lived in McLean and wanted to preserve the Potomac bluffs, slowed the matter to a near halt, saying he would personally have to give written permission for any tree thicker than eight inches to be cut down.[77] The next day, when Interior officials posted signs at Merrywood saying they had acquired a scenic easement on the property preventing further clearing, they were greeted by a front-end loader driver and a pile of burning trees.[78]

But the fight was over. And given how much Jackie had influenced Lafayette Square behind the scenes, it is possible that she had a hand in this one, too. Acknowledging it was a losing battle, the developer would sell the property for $650,000 in 1964 to Wyatt Dickerson, who moved into Merrywood with his wife, Nancy, the CBS (and later NBC) newswoman who was friendly with Udall. By 1968, Dickerson had figured out a solution: build clustered townhomes that preserved much of the woods. The idea was approved and the project completed. Meanwhile, Nancy Dickerson needed some decorating help for Merrywood. She knew just whom to call: Sister Parish.[79]

Although Jackie had completed most of the White House restoration, she felt there was still much to be done. But fate intervened. In her final hours as a resident of the White House, in a haze of sadness, Jackie was readying to leave her home of the last one thousand days. There was so much unfinished. Every breath felt incomplete. President Kennedy's vision for the New Frontier—its light was gone.

Jackie's work—indeed her entire life—had also been up-ended by his wrenching death. And whether she was conscious of its symbolism or not, she needed to complete one final personal touch before leaving the White House for good. She called the executive mansion's painter, Joseph Karitas, the man who had helped decorate Caroline's chest of drawers with stripes. "Can you please come up to the second floor?" she asked him.

He found her standing there, with her sister, Lee, and West, the usher, in front of a large oil painting that was damaged with scaling, exposing the canvas. Karitas sidled up to her before the painting, and noticed that its gold frame was also badly scarred.

"Look at it," she begged. "Can you please fix it? Mrs. Johnson is moving into the White House this afternoon. I want it to look nice for her."

Karitas went down and got his paint and art brushes. He began painting the picture, filling in the image where the paint had been knocked off the canvas. Then he touched up the gold frame. Jackie watched from a chair and then encouraged a little mischief.

"Joe, Mr. West said you should paint some Indians in the picture while you're painting there." He went along with the gag, hoping it would cheer her up. He knew how she felt.[80]

Jackie then told Karitas to sign his name on the bottom. He obliged.

In the days and months after she left the White House, she again turned to Warnecke for help—and more. "Rosebowl" had earned Jackie's respect as an architect and a person, and she repaid him with yet another historic commission: to design the president's gravesite at Arlington National Cemetery, a prominent slope of grass, with white stones set in the earth and an eternal flame—a monumental exercise in restraint.[81]

Grand Central was anything but minimalist. Its size and scope were monuments to industrialism, and in its smallest architectural details the space offered visual gifts to those who took time to notice. Jackie appreciated good design no matter what the form, so she was prepared to dive into the scrum of yet another preservation struggle, most likely thinking about her other decade-old accomplishments and hoping to keep her winning streak alive.

Jackie entered the vaulted concourse of Grand Central on January 30, 1975, wearing a tan dress, gold chain, and her trademark Cartier watch beneath her coat and scarf. She had arrived by cab promptly for the morning press conference—just as Kent Barwick had hoped—alone, as usual, with no security trailing behind her. Inside, as her suede bootheels clicked across the marble floors, an old feeling stirred within her. She was inspired to erase the grime, to uncover the gem of this Beaux-Arts beauty in the same way she had been moved to free the White House of its dowdy Eisenhower furnishings, to stop the bulldozers in Lafayette Square, and to silence the saws at Merrywood.

She walked from the concourse down the ramp leading to the Oyster Bar, Grand Central's lower-level restaurant. The Oyster Bar, as old as the terminal, had offered to host the event, not just for the short-term publicity but as an act of self preservation, knowing construction would surely disrupt or kill its business. The Municipal Art Society, after a frenzied week of preparations, agreed that the location would be perfect, a place that spoke to tradition and fond memories.

In the left-side area of the catacomb-like space, staff had set up a banquet table near the bar that was already filled with oysters. A breakfast spread of bagels and coffee was next to it. The table was long enough to seat about a dozen members of the Committee to Save Grand Central, a gilt group that was only partially in attendance. Committee chairman Robert F. Wagner Jr., who had created the Landmarks Preservation Commission in 1965 when he was mayor of New York, was getting married that day and missed the event.

As Jackie entered the room, she saw other notable New Yorkers preparing to take their seats, including Bess Myerson, who was both the first Jewish Miss America and the city's former commissioner of Consumer Affairs; *New Yorker* writer and man-about-town Brendan Gill; Hughdie's grandnephew, Louis Auchincloss, president of the Museum of the City of

New York; architect Philip Johnson; and Manhattan borough president and civil rights activist Percy E. Sutton.[82] Overall, the committee had some ninety members, mostly East Coast elites, including writer George Plimpton, Jackie's friend who had been standing next to Sirhan Sirhan when the assassin pulled the trigger on Bobby Kennedy.

The event had been carefully planned for the morning in order to give the television crews time to run their stories for the noon and evening broadcasts. Radio had the whole day to run the report. And even international newspapers such as the *Times* of London were able to meet their deadlines for the next day. The seating was also arranged to highlight the guest of honor; she had just arrived. The space, which can seat 250 people, was jammed with supporters and media from around the world, and they had really only come to hear what Jackie had to say. The crowded space buzzed with anticipation.

Jackie's seat was in the middle of the table, befitting her status as the star. But she, like everyone else there, knew that she did not need the press coverage, she was *giving* it. As she took off her black cloth coat and scarf and settled into the seat, her eyes noted the details of the room—the vaulted ceiling, the coziness of the subterranean space, the blue-check tablecloths, the bank of cameras before her, and the reporters stuffed in every nook, some on bended knee before her.[83] Kent Barwick, as head of the Municipal Art Society, took his seat beside her, but in a last-minute dash to take care of some details, he stood up and lost his spot to then congressman Ed Koch—who understood that

January 30, 1975. Jackie at the Oyster Bar press conference to save Grand Central Terminal. *(Bettman/CORBIS)*

not only were there millions of eyeballs on the event but there were also millions of dollars on the line. He had never seen press interest like this before and he knew he was part of something big. He noted to himself that this could be a case important enough to go all the way to the Supreme Court.[84]

Against another wall, the group had hung a bedsheet, the backdrop for a slide projection that would "educate" the media about the importance of Grand Central. The concept was the brainchild of Frederic Papert, another former advertising executive who had done advance work for Bobby Kennedy's presidential campaign. Aside from knowing Jackie well, he had joined MAS as president after creating New York's Carnegie Hill Historic District in the early 1970s.

There must have been a twinge between Papert and Jackie when they saw each other that morning. They both knew a thing or two about campaigns—how to motivate the public, how to use the media, and how to influence the influencers—but here they were, trying one last time to win, not for a Kennedy, but for the soul of a city.

Papert had assigned the slide show to Hugh Hardy, a young sole-practice architect who had grown up in nearby Westchester County and had taken the train to Grand Central as often as he could as a young teenager, enthralled by the sight of the platforms sparkling from the ice chips used to wash them down. Where else could you come to a city with sparkling platforms? With stars twinkling in the ceiling? He had volunteered to join the fight to save the terminal before knowing who else was on the committee. When he heard Jackie was involved, he didn't say, "Oh, wow, this was the most amazing thing ever," which he later admitted it turned out to be. He was surprised that when she talked to him she talked to *him*—a trait that is rare in New York. There was no aura to penetrate. She was right there.[85]

With everyone seated, the lights dimmed for Hardy's show, and waiters who had been preparing the room for lunch stopped working and lined the walls to watch.

The twenty-minute slide show used old photographs from books and the MAS archives to show the history of Grand Central, its complex engineering and design that allowed for a mix of pedestrians, real estate, cars, and short- and long-distance trains all coming together in a seamless, functional design.

"It represents one of the greatest success stories of architecture and planning in the world," Hardy told the room, clicking through the images. "We intend to demonstrate that Grand Central can again function as the symbol, marketplace and economic engine, with which a preeminently important part of midtown Manhattan can be rejuvenated."[86]

Like a maestro in the dark, Hardy was finding a special way to move the crowd, helping them understand that this was an extraordinary place that was threatened, a place a hundred times superior and far more important than Penn Station ever was because it was an integral part of the city. When Hardy was done, the room cheered.

Then the lights came up. Bess Myerson read a statement

from Wagner, who explained that the committee had plenty of private attorneys "standing ready to support the city's case with a 'friend of the court' brief," words that would make it more difficult for Mayor Beame to find excuses about appealing, especially if it would cost the city money. Beame, struggling to manage a metropolis heading toward bankruptcy, was in the midst of laying off teachers and trash collectors,[87] so it would have been politically acceptable for him to explain that New York was too broke to fight the railroad. Wagner did not want to give him that chance, saying the Committee to Save Grand Central was going to "sound an alarm in New York and across the country that the battle against the thoughtless waste of our manmade environment is farther from being won than many of us had thought. What's at issue here is the very concept of landmark preservation."[88]

After Myerson finished reading the statement, Philip Johnson, tall and bespectacled, an architectural rival of Breuer's, and one of the key voices behind the failed attempt to save Penn Station, stepped to the microphone. "Europe has its cathedrals and we have Grand Central Station," Johnson said. "Europe wouldn't put a tower on a cathedral."

The audience cheered again and then fell silent, except for some clinking of dishes and silverware in the kitchen, as Jackie began to speak.

"If we don't care about our past we can't have very much hope for our future," she said into a bank of microphones and over the din of flashbulbs popping. "We've all heard that it's

January 30, 1975. Architect Philip Johnson (at left with glasses), Jackie, Bess Myerson, and Ed Koch, leaving the Oyster Bar press conference, with Grand Central Terminal in the backdrop. *(Bettman/CORBIS)*

too late, or that it has to happen, that it's inevitable. But I don't think that's true. Because I think if there is a great effort, even if it's the eleventh hour, then you can succeed and I know that's what we'll do." [89]

Her words, which she had written herself, were sparse. She knew from her political experiences that if she delivered a forty-five-minute speech it would lose its effectiveness and she would have a greater chance of being misquoted. Deliver a sound bite just right and the press had to use it. They had nothing else.

Before Jackie left, Beckelman brought her over to meet the waiters and chefs. She shook hands with all of them, one of whom had taken JFK's order there years before.

"He ordered two glasses of milk and a cup of custard," the waiter fondly recalled on the spot. "He gave me a dollar but I lost the dollar."[90]

She smiled at him and turned to walk back up to the daylight of the city with Koch, Johnson, and Myerson. Outside, photographers ran past the group, turned on them, and walked backward as they focused their lenses on Jackie's face in front of Grand Central: one icon playing off of the other.

The next day, the papers everywhere were filled with pictures of Jackie, Myerson, Koch, and Johnson walking south on Park Avenue, with Grand Central behind—the perfect photo op. Jackie had generated so much coverage that the committee's volunteer public relations agency, J. Walter Thompson, pinned up clips in its conference room covering all four walls with articles from small-town papers and large-scale dailies around the globe, including those from Europe.

No doubt, Onassis saw the papers and read what Jackie had been doing. With his glasses on, if he looked closely, he could see in the photo's background the giant carved mythical figures that topped the terminal—Mercury (the god of travel), Hercules (labor), and Minerva (knowledge). He called Jackie on Sunday from his villa in the Athens suburb of Glyfada—directly beneath the flight path of many of his own airplanes landing in Athens—and complained of being alone.[91]

While Onassis's health continued to deteriorate, the Municipal Art Society stepped up its efforts to succeed, asking the *Times* to cover the story in greater detail, enlisting Ed Koch to complain to the US secretary of transportation, and forming a quiet alliance with the sympathetic Metropolitan Transit Authority, which leased space at the terminal.[92] But MAS remained very worried about what Beame might do—or more precisely, not do. They needed him to appeal the case.

And so once again, Jackie threw herself into the cause, knowing the battle was at a critical stage. MAS could not lose the momentum coming off of the Oyster Bar press conference, an event that was so successful in making ordinary people suddenly care about preservation that it had instigated a campaign in the Midwest with donors sending in $5 bills to save the station.

Jackie was not afraid to take on people seemingly more powerful than she. And she knew when a fight was worth fighting. After Robert Kennedy's assassination, his wife, Ethel, wanted nuns from her old school to sing at the funeral at St. Patrick's Cathedral in New York. Female voices were not allowed and Leonard Bernstein, who was in charge of the music for the Mass, was told no by the monsignor. Jackie went straight to Archbishop Terence Cooke and said, "This is the way it is going to be." His reply: "Of course."[93]

In addition to being the consummate strategist, she had little patience for process, knowing it could subsume purpose. She was also impatient with the bureaucracy and sluggish pace of committees. She—because of Onassis's grave illness—was running out of time to help Grand Central. She hatched a plan on her own to write to the mayor herself.[94] Surely Beame would be too embarrassed to ignore her pleas and compliments. She did not underestimate the power of her own pen and knew the value of her letters. Those she had written on behalf of the White House restoration had moved people to part with priceless objects. Other notes had helped save Lafayette Square. Her letters sent to friends and strangers alike after JFK's assassination had touched them deeply. Even seemingly inconsequential letters of hers set the world atwitter. A 1964 auction fetched $3,000 for a note she sent in 1955 in response to a man in England suggesting that there were better ways for the Kennedys to spend money than on a $20,000 party. "True, my husband and I are well off," she wrote to the Englishman. "But after taxes household and business expenses and charity, there is not just a great pile of money lying around."[95] The sales price for her letter was nearly double the amount a Martha Washington letter had sold for at that time.

This letter to Beame, though, would be more thought through than the note to the Brit, and would show her now-significant political instincts. She liked strategizing about how to tell the story. In this case, Jackie understood that Beame, in desperate straits politically, needed to be a hero.

She pulled out a sheaf of her trademark blue stationery with the simple 1040 Fifth Avenue engraved at the top. Dated February 24, she wrote the letter longhand, her loopy print leaning slightly to the left. Knowing what she had just been through in

Athens and Paris, the anger, passion, and indeed much of her language in the letter could have reflected how she was feeling about her marriage and Onassis—as well as his decision to divorce her.

Dear Mayor Beame

I write to you about Grand Central Station, with the prayer that you will see fit to have the City of New York appeal Judge Saypol's decision.

Is it not cruel to let our city die by degrees, stripped of all her proud monuments, until there is nothing left of all her history and beauty to inspire our children? If they are not inspired by the past of our city, where will they find the strength to fight for her future?

Americans care about their past, but for short term gain they ignore it and tear down everything that matters.

Maybe, with our bicentennial approaching, this is the moment to take a stand, to reverse the tide, so that we won't all end up in a uniform world of steel and glass boxes.

Old buildings were made better than we will ever be able to afford to make them again. They can have new and useful lives, from the largest to the smallest. They can serve the community and bring people together.

Everyone, from every strata of our city, is wounded by what is happening—but feel powerless—hopeless that their petitions will have any effect.

I think of the time President Kennedy was faced with the

destruction of Lafayette Square, opposite the White House. That
historic 19th century square was about to be demolished to make way
for a huge Eisenhower-approved Government Office Building. All
contracts had been signed. At the last minute he cancelled them—and
as he did so, he said, "This is the act I may be most remembered for."

Dear Mayor Beame—your life has been devoted to this city.
Now you serve her in the highest capacity. You are her people's last
hope—all their last hopes lie with you.

It would be so noble if you were to go down in history as the
man who was brave enough to stem the tide, brave enough to stand
up against the greed that would devour New York bit by bit. People
now, and people not yet born will be grateful to you and honor your
name.

With my admiration and respect
Jacqueline Kennedy Onassis

Beame, a steady man of simple tastes, could have read the
letter seated on a wooden chair with black leather seat pads
in his city hall office, with its flags and fireplace and rich red
drapes, a setting that seemed to exacerbate his stature—just
five foot two. Since his election the year before as the city's first
Jewish mayor, Beame had been mired in New York's calamitous
budget, proving impossible for even a numbers whiz like himself. Beneath his silver hair and furrowed brow, his dark, bushy
eyebrows set off his eyes, focused on this letter, presenting yet
another difficult choice for a leader prone to indecisiveness.
This one was about a building, in the heart of the city, a cause

involving powerful people who could make or break him. The more he considered it, the less choice he seemed to have.

Within a week, Beame announced that his administration would appeal Judge Saypol's decision.

"This case has great significance to the future of preservation in New York City and in the entire United States," Beame said in a press release his office issued. "Grand Central Station was designated a landmark because it is a landmark in every sense of the word; it is a symbol of life in the City of New York . . . Grand Central, like all our landmarks, helps define the greatness of the City. We must work hard to preserve it as part of the integrity of the City of New York." [96]

It was a victory. But for how long? If the case did go to the Supreme Court—a first for a historic preservation issue—every press release, every rally, every call for supporters that MAS would organize would be done to influence public opinion and perhaps those of the judges. Back at 1040 Fifth, smiling at what she had helped achieve, Jackie was already thinking about the composition of the Supreme Court and who might be swayed.

CHAPTER FOUR

The Widow

The day after her phone call from Onassis, Jackie was jolted by another overseas call—from her stepdaughter, Christina. She told Jackie that she had cut short an early February ski trip in Gstaad with her boyfriend because Onassis had collapsed with severe stomach pains. She was keeping vigil with her aunts outside her father's bedroom in Greece, an uncluttered room with few furnishings. He was struggling with the flu and a gallstone attack. Dr. Jacques Caroli, Onassis's personal physician based in Paris, was on his way. Christina said Jackie should come, too.

Jackie jumped on an Olympic Learjet that day, flying with Dr. Isadore Rosenfeld, a New York cardiologist who had treated Onassis the previous November. Rosenfeld was worried that Onassis's heart was too weak to survive the removal of his gallbladder, which Caroli was recommending doing in Paris. As it was, Onassis could barely chew or hold up his head.

When Jackie arrived the next day, she was stunned to see him lying in bed forty pounds lighter and ashen. Outside, the media had been clamoring for hours to know if this was the end for Onassis.

Onassis's sister Merope sent her husband outside to address the reporters.

"He is suffering from influenza with complications but he is resting comfortably now and you can go home," he told them. The reporters, however, knew it was more serious than that, and United Press International (UPI) reported the next day that the myasthenia gravis was threatening his vital organs and endangering his life.[1]

The doctors continued to assert their divergent opinions, as did the family. Christina, who wanted her father to go to Paris to receive what she believed would be the best care, was sobbing over his condition and the stress of having to decide what to do.[2] Onassis, seemingly resigned to die, did not want to go anywhere. But Jackie felt strongly he at least go to Paris.

"He's my husband, and I believe this switch is necessary," said Jackie. "Let's not argue."[3]

Jackie took Onassis, bundled in a heavy overcoat and scarf, to the Athens airport Thursday, where they boarded an Olympic Learjet specially equipped with a bed and medical equipment that had been on the runway on standby for three days.[4] Doctors and his entourage boarded a Boeing 707.[5]

In France, before checking into the hospital, Onassis wanted to spend one last night at his apartment at 88 Avenue Foch, near the Bois de Boulogne. He arrived there by limousine, slumped between Jackie and Christina. Set on one of the city's most prestigious streets, lined with chestnut trees and grand palaces, and occupied by super-rich families such as the Rothschilds, the fifteen-room apartment had romantic views

February 6, 1975. Jackie and Christina arriving at Onassis's apartment in France, after a flight from Athens, the night before he entered the hospital. *(Bettman/CORBIS)*

of the Arc de Triomphe and the Eiffel Tower.[6] And on this day, the entrance was swarming with shouting paparazzi when he arrived. Onassis looked gaunt, his silver hair greased back, black-as-night arching eyebrows framing his bugged-out eyes, his large nose further exaggerated by weight loss. Still fiercely proud, he insisted on walking in unaided.[7]

"I don't want those sons of bitches to see me being held up by a couple of women," he snarled.[8]

Jackie stayed at the apartment that night while Christina—who knew of her father's plans to divorce—took a room at the Plaza Athénée.[9] Onassis settled in to his large bedroom on the fifth floor. The room had a stone fireplace, an antique brass bed, and family photographs. There were red velvet drapes, a gilt dressing screen, and fake Watteau paintings on gray silk walls. On his nightstand were a crucifix and a calculator. He put on blue silk pajamas and a robe custom-made by Lanvin.[10] But he moaned through the night, struggling to get comfortable enough to sleep.[11]

The next day guards drove him in a Peugeot from the apartment's underground garage to the hospital, and he settled in a spacious room in the more modern wing named after Eisenhower, the thought of whom would have reminded Jackie of her painful preinaugural tour of the White House, as well as the threat to Lafayette Square.[12]

On February 9, surgeons removed his gallbladder.

"It was a small operation and now he is feeling much better," Onassis's right-hand man, Johnny Meyer, told a press

February 7, 1975. Onassis arrives at American Hospital in Paris.
(Richard Melloul/Sygma/CORBIS)

conference at the hospital. "He can stand up. That's all I can say." [13]

In truth, there were complications. Onassis developed hepatitis and pneumonia. He was on massive doses of antibiotics and staff fed him intravenously while he was on a respirator in the intensive care unit. [14] Over the next week, the hospital issued a statement downgrading his status to "guarded." [15] The Onassis women held vigil, with Jackie avoiding the hospital room when Christina was there, and vice versa. When Onassis was awake for brief moments, he spoke mostly Greek. [16]

Jackie visited him daily, but the intensive care unit restricted visiting hours. In her free time, she went to Notre

Dame, lit a candle, and said a prayer for her husband. She also visited the Louvre, the Orangerie, the hairdresser, and shopped, with the retail therapy going especially deep at Ungaro.[17]

Ten days after the surgery, Onassis remained unconscious but his condition had stabilized. Doctors told Jackie—away from her kids for nearly three weeks—that it was safe to fly home. But before she left by Olympic Learjet on February 19, she consulted with a trusted physician in New York who told her she should stay. Onassis's condition was grave, and the whole world was watching, he said. She ignored his advice. John, always a rascal, was fourteen, and in New York alone with only secret service agents and their longtime governess and cook, Marta Sgubin, watching over him. It was also the season for him to visit boarding schools he might attend the following year. Caroline, reserved and mature for her age, was a senior at Concord Academy, a boarding school outside of Boston. On top of Jackie needing to be with John, a documentary that Caroline had worked on about Tennessee coal miners was airing on NBC.[18] Caroline had traveled in the summer of 1973 to the Appalachian community with a high school friend after learning about it through the Robert F. Kennedy Memorial Foundation, which was funding an oral history project led by a New York nun. Jackie didn't want to miss the documentary's debut and she planned to host a party in her daughter's honor.[19]

Back at her apartment in New York, Jackie immediately called the hospital to check on Onassis. Artemis, the sister-in-law with whom Jackie was closest, said his condition was unchanged.

Jackie's apartment at 1040 Fifth Avenue had the classic look inside and out of a prewar building: large windows, detailed moldings, nickel fixtures, arched doorways. After deciding she could no longer live in Washington after the assassination because tourists were so aggressive that they picnicked outside the home where she and the kids stayed, this home felt pleasantly familiar to her. It was designed in the 1920s by Rosario Candela, the same man who did 740 Park, her grandfather's apartment building where she had lived as a girl. The apartment at 1040 Fifth, part of a stately limestone building, had cost her

February 13, 1975. Jackie leaving the hospital in Paris. *(Bettman/CORBIS)*

$200,000, an enormous sum in 1964.[20] It had five bathrooms and five bedrooms,[21] and black-and-white marble flooring greeted guests as they stepped off the private elevator directly into her fifteenth-floor home. The large, square, paneled living room with parquet floors and tall French windows, dressed by the famous drapery master John Fowler, could have felt stiff with art by John Singer Sargent, velvet Louis XVI chairs, and Roman sculptures of Hercules and a boy's head, both of which JFK had bought in Italy for his wife. But John's drum kit kept it real, along with a world map covered with pins that showed where Jack had traveled during his presidency. From the living room, she enjoyed the view of the Central Park Reservoir and the Metropolitan Museum of Art, watching the people below through a telescope.[22]

She was there, in her home, on Saturday, March 15, 1975. When the phone rang just after 7:30 AM, she heard the news from Artemis: Onassis had taken a turn for the worse. Jackie made immediate plans to leave. Before she could get to the airport, Artemis called again.

"He's dead," she said. "Christina was with him when he left us."[23]

The loftily named Aristotle Socrates Onassis, short and square with black eyes and a shock of silver hair, was consumed by pneumonia and took his last breath in American Hospital in Paris.

Although many reported him to be six years younger because he had lied about his age for so long, he was seventy-five,

Jackie just forty-five. She was not there to cradle his head, to watch his final breath, or to hear his last words. She did not call the priest to administer last rites. In more ways than one, there was an ocean between them, more awkward than ever, and Jackie knew that she must cross it one last time, in spectacular fashion, for his funeral.

She hung up the phone, called her sister Lee, and told her not to come to the funeral. Funerals were one thing whose stagecraft Jackie was an expert in and the last thing anyone wanted was the media bringing up the old story about her sister's relationship with Onassis, which had happened before Jackie's engagement to, him.

The next call went to her brother-in-law Ted Kennedy, who had assumed a paternalistic role after Bobby's assassination and remained a close confidant to Jackie. Ted would meet her in Paris. She also phoned Nancy Tuckerman, who agreed to meet her at the airport for the next Air France flight out.[24] Finally, she called her mother, and arranged for her to bring her kids on a separate flight.

But Jackie had one other person to tell—a guest in her house. The documentary film that Caroline had been working on was under the watch of producer Karen Lerner, the ex-wife of Alan Jay Lerner, who had written the musical *Camelot*. Indeed, this was the same Camelot that had been the inspiration for the Kennedy presidential myth, a concept that Jackie herself had applied in an interview a week after her husband's assassination. Karen Lerner had slept at Jackie's the previous night in preparation for the film's debut and the party Jackie had planned to host the next night. Lerner was still there, in the room where Onassis had typically stayed, when Jackie came in and said, "Ari's dead. I'm going to Paris, so you stay here and be the hostess . . . I don't want anything to disturb this—it's for Caroline and I just want it to go ahead."[25]

Then Jackie dressed for mourning, again, this time in a black turtleneck sweater, skirt, stockings, and shoes, topped with a black leather trench coat cinched at the waist, looking

March 15, 1975. Jackie, barely visible in the scrum and wearing sunglasses, leaves her New York apartment for Paris, where Onassis had died earlier that day. *(Ron Galella)*

March 15, 1975. Jackie leaves 1040 Fifth Avenue for the airport on the day Onassis died. *(Ron Galella/WireImage)*

more like a chic urbanite than a devastated widow. It was a long day, stuck in her apartment, with a throng of media outside, waiting for her to leave for the overnight flight to Paris.

When it was finally time to go in the early evening, she stepped onto the elevator. To brace herself for a crush of cameras, she slid on her oversize sunglasses, despite the day's last light at just past 6:00 PM. While the glasses covered much of her face, they could not hide everything. Some of the hundred gawkers and journalists on the sidewalk clustered around the canopy at 1040 saw a faint, odd smirk on her face. For a woman whose stoicism and perfect manners defined the most public and analyzed funeral of the twentieth century—that of John F. Kennedy—people wondered if her smile was the mask of shock, a reflexive, almost embarrassed pose, or a signal to the world that she had finally been liberated.

Escorted by four uniformed New York City policemen and four secret service agents, the brisk wind tussled her center-part hair. The sidewalk was so packed that she could not have noticed Ron Galella, the stalking paparazzo she had sued in 1972; he was maintaining his court-ordered twenty-five-foot distance from her.

Galella focused his lens on her, noting what a "madhouse" it was, and watching as she pushed her way through the crowd before she disappeared.[26]

The chauffeur drove away to the airport named after Jackie's first husband.[27] The grin did not fade as she left. When she arrived at the airport, she was escorted directly to the gate and boarded the plane.

There is nothing quite like the darkness over the Atlantic Ocean in the middle of the night. And as Jackie hurtled through it on Air France flight 070, she had to prepare for what she would say to the world about the loss of another husband. Thankfully, she was good at conjuring quotes for speeches or finding the right words about death. She had given many suggestions to JFK and RFK over the years, including the Shakespeare quote that Bobby read at Jack's funeral:

When he shall die
Take him and cut him out in little stars
And he will make the face of heaven so fine
That all the world will be in love with night
And pay no worship to the garish sun.

Her words for Ari would surely be a lot less poetic.

France is a country that loved her as much as she loved it. After her junior year abroad studying at the University of Grenoble and the Sorbonne, and her special summer with Lee, Jackie's next trip to Paris happened a decade later when she returned with President Kennedy on his first state trip to the continent. For the presidential gala there, she wore a simple sheaf gown adorned with pink-and-white lace creatively made of raffia. She lit up the room. Or, as one writer said about that evening, "Truly la vie was very much en rose."[28] The next night, at a state dinner at Versailles, she wore a Givenchy gown with a cream robe, prompting Charles de Gaulle to say she belonged in a Watteau painting.[29] With her command of the language and knowledge of French culture, she interpreted de Gaulle for her husband, who acknowledged his wife's popularity there by saying, "I do not think it altogether inappropriate to introduce myself to this audience. I am the man who accompanied Jacqueline Kennedy to Paris, and I have enjoyed it."

That was then.

Now, Jackie knew that the French, like the rest of the world, were wondering why she was not at Onassis's side when he died.

Her plane landed in Paris at 7:00 AM. She made no statement, waited in the VIP lounge while customs handled passport formalities, and then a chauffeur drove her to 88 Avenue Foch. There, she shut herself in from the media horde and let most of the day pass. At 5:15 she emerged, accompanied by Onassis's private nurse, Monique Clouthier, an imposing bodyguard, and her sisters-in-law Artemis and Kalliroi.[30] The group left for American Hospital, where her husband's body was laid out on a bier in a hospital chapel, surrounded by white flowers.

Christina had been at her father's side since Friday and into Saturday, when he died. But she was not at the hospital when Jackie arrived Sunday evening. The two were not friendly, not from the very beginning. In fact, Christina and her brother had cried during the reception on the yacht after their father's wedding to Jackie, the siblings clinging to the childish fantasy that their divorced parents would reunite. But Christina was not just avoiding her stepmother at the hospital. She was devastated. Indeed her life was a Greek tragedy. In 1946, Onassis had married Athina (Tina) Livanos, the teenage daughter of shipping magnate Stavros Livanos—Onassis's industrial rival. Tina divorced him in 1960 after catching him having sex with Callas in the saloon of the yacht. Tina then married Stavros Niarchos— another shipping rival—whose previous wife, Eugenia, was Tina's sister. Eugenia had recently died of a suspicious overdose. With her mother married to her uncle, Christina—who battled weight problems, dressed sloppily, and was woefully insecure about her relationships and appearance—now had to endure an international fashion icon for a stepmother, leaving the young woman to feel even worse about herself (despite constant dieting and a nose job). Christina, of course, also had assumed that Jackie was a gold digger. Then, in the last two years, another string of tragedies pushed her to the brink. Her mother and brother dead, she had married California real estate broker Joseph Bolker and divorced him within a nine-month period after her father threatened to cut her out of his will over the relationship. But Christina had reconciled with Onassis.[31] Now both men in her life were gone.

Jackie, in her leather trench, looked like a very different widow this time. She wore no hat or veil as she pushed through the heavy bronze doors of the hospital's chilly chapel where Onassis's body laid with a Greek Orthodox icon on his chest and flowers, including the orchid she had sent. She spent fifteen minutes with the body.[32]

The last time she had knelt before a husband's bier, it was in the East Room of the White House, at 4:00 AM, immediately after Jack's body had been transferred from the naval hospital. A priest had said a few words and there were white candles around the casket, along with Kennedy's closest associates. Jackie approached the casket, buried her head in the flag, and then left after a few moments.[33] Jackie had begun visualizing JFK's funeral on the Air Force One flight back from Dallas, directing even the smallest details that would be meaningful, such as having military cadets, with whom the president had been impressed on a trip to Ireland, lay a wreath. She told Bobby to check a guidebook on Lincoln's funeral for answers about the lying-in-state process. And she had the White House upholsterer use the black cambric fabric he would typically apply as a finishing touch on the bottom of a chair to drape over the windows, mantels, and chandeliers. There was plenty of it to hang and the upholsterer and his wife worked through the night to get it done before Jackie and the president's body arrived.[34]

For RFK's funeral, besides ensuring that Ethel had the nuns she had requested singing at the Mass, Jackie noticed that Bobby's casket was only inches off the floor of the funeral train car as it traveled between New York and Washington. With so many people coming to the tracks along the route to pay their respects, she asked for help in raising the casket. "It should be elevated so that the crowds of people watching the train might have the chance to see it," she implored one man on the train.[35]

But Jackie did not need to bother herself with the funeral details of her now late husband; those were being handled by the Onassis clan and his loyal associates. As she left the hospital chapel, escorted again by the nurse and the bodyguard, she put her glasses back on and knew that this time she would not be stage crafting the event. She simply needed to show up at the same chapel on Skorpios where they had been married not quite seven years before.

———

While Jackie and Onassis had pulled away from each other toward the end, Christina's relationship with her father had become closer. They had nothing left but each other. Having been there when he died, Christina, twenty-four, refused to leave his body on the flight from Paris to Aktion, near Skorpios, where he would be buried. Jackie, Ted Kennedy, and the three Onassis sisters had flown ahead and were waiting on the

March 18, 1975. Jackie walks with Christina, followed by Senator Edward M. Kennedy, as they leave an Olympic Airlines plane carrying Onassis's body. *(Bettman/CORBIS)*

tarmac to greet the casket and a heavily sedated Christina. As Christina descended the plane steps, Jackie approached her and gently held her hand. Fragile under the best of circumstances, Christina was weeping, her black hair flying in the wind, her skin a yellow hue.[36]

"Why are all these people around us? Get them away," she demanded.

"Take it easy now," Jackie told her. "It will soon be over."[37]

Separately, the Kennedy children and their grandmother Janet had arrived in Aktion, and from there everyone drove in limos to Nydri, a tiny fishing village, before transferring by boat to Skorpios. It was a cool, wet day—March 18, 1975.

John, fourteen, and Caroline, seventeen, in jeans and sweaters, drove a golf cart around Skorpios, reminiscing about happier times there: his speedboat, her white pony, fishing trips, long days under the sun with their cousins. But they could hear the hum and chop of boats and helicopters bringing mourners and the unwelcomed media to the private island. Now it was time for them to head to their guesthouse to change into more appropriate funeral attire—a blue blazer and tie for him and a blue sweater and gray skirt for her—and head for the dock. There was nothing left to do but wait there with their grandmother for the cabin cruiser containing the casket that held Onassis. Among those waiting were Onassis's little dog, Vana, a stray that had attached herself to the magnate and always had a sixth sense about his arrival on Skorpios.[38]

In the distance was the *Christina*, with its anchor down. Its

March 18, 1975. Jackie's mother, Janet Auchincloss (left), with John Jr., Caroline, and several others, awaiting the arrival of Onassis's body on Skorpios. *(Bettman/CORBIS)*

flag was at half-mast. The crew wore black. The Skorpios chapel's bell tolled.

In the months leading up to this day, Onassis's zest and sturdy body had been slowly diminished by his disease, which forced him to clip tape or the adhesive strips from Band-Aids and tack them onto his eyelids to hold them open. He had also been suddenly ravaged by the right-left-right punches of flu, pneumonia, and gallbladder surgery, from which he never recovered.

And here he was, on his last journey to Skorpios from American Hospital in Paris. A second launch carried Jackie,

Senator Ted Kennedy, Christina, and his three sisters. Other mourners were arriving by ferry.

A light rain fell as John and Caroline stood on the dock, waiting to greet their mother and say good-bye to her husband one final time.

Jackie was a widow again. After Kennedy's soul-crushing death, and then the devastating back-to-back murders of Martin Luther King and Robert Kennedy in 1968, capping a decade of despair, she seemed to take this funeral in stride. Disembarking onto Skorpios still wearing the black leather trench coat and her fly-eye sunglasses, this death, with this husband, had been long and slow, and she was as ready as she could ever be.

"A widow for a second time," whispered one old woman in a black shawl as the funeral procession walked by. Others whispered about a curse that Jackie had brought on the Onassis family—and whether Maria Callas would be coming.[39]

Once again, what appeared to be a Mona Lisa smile swept beneath Jackie's glasses.[40]

The village priest led the six pallbearers some two hundred yards up the hill toward the chapel, with about sixty mourners trailing slowly behind. The procession's pecking order was clear. Jackie held John's arm. Caroline stood between her mother and her uncle Ted, who was wearing a navy blue trench. Christina walked ahead of all of them—closest to the casket—surrounded by her aunts, arm in arm, an old Greek custom, though it looked as if they were forming a wall to block out Jackie and her children.[41]

March 18, 1875. Onassis's funeral procession to the chapel on Skorpios. Christina Onassis, center front, surrounded by her aunts; second row: John Jr., Jackie, Caroline, and Ted Kennedy. *(Bettman/CORBIS)*

The chapel courtyard was lined with hundreds of white lilies in pots draped with red velvet. There were seven large wreaths on white tripods outside the chapel. Set in theatrical and coordinating fashion against the dazzling pink blossoms of cherry trees on the terraced hillside behind the Chapel of the Little Virgin, one of the wreaths, made of white and pink carnations, pink hyacinths, and white lilies had a banner across it that read: TO ARI FROM JACKIE. Four other wreaths were from a Swiss bank.

Not all of the sixty invited mourners could squeeze into the eighteenth-century chapel. And Onassis employees—gardeners, domestics, and sailors—each in job-specific uniforms, huddled near the entrance holding candles. Inside, the walls were lined with decorative columns and arched niches painted sky blue. Greek Orthodox priest Zavitsanos Apostolous, with his thick black beard, black cap, and ceremonial robe, read from St. Paul's Epistle to the Thessalonians. A small choir sang in verse: "I went to the grave and saw the naked bones, and I said to myself, who are you? King or soldier? Rich or poor? Sinner or just?"

One of Onassis's sisters rushed out of the chapel, overwhelmed with grief.

"Come and give him your last kiss," Father Apostolous said to those before him, prompting the tradition of mourners to touch their lips to an icon on top of the simple wooden coffin. One by one, they did, each leaving a white flower on top. When it was Christina's turn, she shook and swayed, and was helped back to her seat. Jackie, who appeared drawn but tearless, stepped forward, kissed the oak lid, and bid him good-bye.

Beyond that, there was no eulogy. Onassis did not want one. When the funeral was over, pallbearers carried the coffin by its four silver handles and placed it on a concrete sarcophagus beneath a cypress tree to the left of the chapel, opposite the grave of his son. Alexander Onassis had died at age twenty-five when his Piaggio plane, part of Onassis's Olympic Airways fleet, had dipped its right wing just after takeoff and dived into the runway. The freakish loss of his only son had plagued the millionaire with a deep depression—many believed it was then that he lost his will to live—and the suspicion that an enemy had fatally rigged the aircraft.[42]

Onassis had chosen this grave site for himself shortly after Alexander died, telling one adviser to leave the cypress tree there and giving very specific instructions to pass along to the architect.[43]

March 18, 1975. Christina Onassis and her aunt say a final good-bye to Aristotle. Jackie stands to the left of Caroline. *(Bettman/CORBIS)*

As Jackie stepped out of the chapel following the coffin, which had his name and the face of his patron saint on it, she slipped on her sunglasses even though the skies had darkened further, the clouds releasing a few big drops. The priest said more prayers and a dazed Christina tossed some dirt on the coffin as it was lowered into the vault. Jackie's face crumpled. With quivering lips, she struggled to stay composed.[44]

But she would soon recover.

After Onassis's funeral, she returned to Athens, stayed a few days with Artemis, and then boarded the plane for home. But before she did so, Jackie granted a brief interview with an Athens newspaper: "Aristotle Onassis rescued me at a moment when my life was engulfed with shadows," she said, with flashbulbs popping. "He meant a lot to me. He brought me into a world where one could find both happiness and love. We lived through many beautiful experiences together which cannot be forgotten, and for which I will be eternally grateful."[45]

CHAPTER FIVE

The Target

Back in New York, Jackie checked in almost daily with Artemis to see how she was doing and, more subtly, to check on Christina's mood. After all, her stepdaughter would be the one to determine whether there would be a battle over the estate. When Jackie married Onassis, she had asked the federal government to stop the regular payments that had begun after the assassination. Financial support from the Kennedy family also ended with her marriage to Onassis. Although the children had trust funds, Jackie had a lifestyle to maintain and no active income. No job. Still, Jackie never wanted a public catfight over money. Christina knew it—and sharpened her claws. She instructed one of her father's henchmen to leak a story—a big story—that would embarrass the widow and make it impossible for her to demand a big number.

Jackie, who always canceled her newspaper and magazine subscriptions around assassination anniversaries or salacious book releases so she did not have to relive her tragedies or read unflattering stories, must have been blindsided on April 12, 1975, when she picked up her *New York Times*. There, on the front page, was a bold scoop by John Corry with a double-deck headline: ONASSIS SAID TO HAVE PLANNED DIVORCE, PROVIDED $3-MILLION FOR WIDOW IN WILL. That the article was in the paper of record, one that did not have a gossip column, gave the story credibility. The article contradicted earlier reports circulating for months that said she could receive up to $200 million after his death. Corry also reported the secret discussions with Roy Cohn the previous December, when Onassis asked him to begin divorce proceedings, saying that Onassis only dropped the issue because his health had rapidly deteriorated.

The story was not only embarrassing and infuriating, but the timing was horrible. The Municipal Art Society had planned an enormous concert rally for later that week at Grand Central, where organizers would unveil the campaign's slogan—"No more bites out of the Big Apple"—with Benny Goodman and Dick Cavett, among others. Now she could not attend without becoming a distraction.[1] She was also set to leave for Greece the next week, on April 20, to attend a service on Skorpios marking the end of the forty-day Greek Orthodox mourning period.

Jackie demanded that Christina issue a denial of the report.

Christina, still in Paris, was not yet fluent in handling the sort of high-profile public negotiations that her father had been expert in; she broke quickly and issued a statement saying her father's marriage indeed had been a happy one and "all rumors of intended divorce are untrue." Christina also denied that she and Jackie were arguing over the will.[2]

The *New York Times* story prompted *Washington Post* columnist Jack Anderson to finally publish the story Onassis had given him months before about Jackie's spending. MRS. ONASSIS SELLS USED WARDROBE, the headline tattled, going on to say, "Associates recall hearing Onassis gripe about a $9,000 bill for gowns from Valentino's of Rome. 'What does she do with all the clothes,' he exploded. 'I never see her in anything but blue jeans.'"[3]

Reselling clothes was not new for Jackie. She would trade suits, gowns, blouses, pants, purses—some of which were never used and some of which were designed by Halston, Valentino, or Yves Saint Laurent—for cash. One favorite resale shop was Encore in Manhattan. While in the White House, she would have resale commission checks sent to her secretary, Mary Gallagher, who kept the books for the couple. Jackie's clothing was resold under Gallagher's name and the Encore checks would be sent to the secretary's home; she'd deposit the funds and then repay Jackie.

Jackie was outraged by the media frenzy but she left for Greece to attend Onassis's final service, leaving her mother to deal with the Associated Press reporter who tracked her down at home in Washington. Janet rarely spoke publicly about her daughter. But this time, she unleashed.

"There was never any question of divorce," Janet told the media. "All marriages have their spots and they came from very different backgrounds and countries. They had their difficult moments as you and I have probably had . . . Obviously there was a good difference in ages. She had children in this country. He didn't want to be in this country very much, and they lived a life where they came and went when either one of them wanted to see the other one. It's difficult being married to somebody who has a very strong character with whom you had little in common through the years when you were growing up, when you come from a different country with different customs and ideas . . . But whose business is it besides your own? If you have enough sense and dignity to work it out between you . . . Actually I think she's going to miss him very much, at least she told me she was."

Rumors of divorce, Janet added, "just make me sick." [4]

When Jackie landed in Athens to mark the end of the mourning, the strain of all she had been through this year showed when she walked off the plane. She looked thin and pale, exacerbated by the tradition of not wearing makeup or jewelry during that period of grief.

Artemis, the oldest of the Onassis sisters, and the one who was closest with Aristotle, brought Jackie back to her villa for the night. Christina purposely stayed away. The next day, waiting in the Olympic Airways' VIP lounge for a plane to Skorpios, employees came to greet her. Jackie greeted them warmly by name, held their hands, and thanked them for their sympathy.[5]

Once they were all on the ground in Skorpios, Christina tried her best to be courteous, kissing Jackie on each cheek and asking her how she was doing. Artemis was pleased to see the two had put their differences aside for the day, even issuing a joint statement that said, "It is the desire of Miss Christina Onassis, and she understands it to also be the desire of Mrs. Jacqueline Onassis, that they both be left at peace and all detrimental and harmful speculations cease."

In the chapel, a village priest swung an incense-filled censer while Jackie, Christina, and a handful of close friends and relatives offered prayers. Mourners completed the rite by eating a bread loaf that weighed forty-four pounds, a symbolic act meant to launch his soul.[6] During the ceremony, Jackie accepted the holy water from the priest and held Artemis's hand. The women whispered to each other. Christina, sitting to the right of Jackie, was averting her eyes. Jackie could not help but look at Christina.[7]

When the ceremony was over, most of the forty guests left the island.[8] Jackie walked to the pink house to gather her belongings, passing through the lush and private gardens before entering the first floor. There, she took in each room with its unique view of the Ionian Sea. On the first floor, she stood in the spacious bedroom, where she and Onassis had slept in a large bed with mosquito netting. There was a big bathroom, a kitchen filled with blue stemware and local pottery, and a living room with a fireplace surrounded by decorative tiles. The sofa, covered in a small floral print, was positioned in front of the fireplace at Onassis's request so he could nap. There were plants in every room, lavish paintings and antiques from expensive stores in London and Athens, vases with orchids and wildflowers, everything kept in perfect order by the *Christina*'s staff. On the second floor, reached by a small staircase, she swept through the guest bedroom and bathroom one last time. The cool terracotta tiles throughout the house were covered with thick traditional Greek flokati rugs, their shaggy wool fibers in shades of cream and beige.

Decorating the space—as Jackie had done with the White House—had become an almost curatorial obsession as she tried to adhere to the traditions of a typical Mykonos house. And when she completed the interior, she turned her attention outside, tearing down a high solid wall around the garden in exchange for a more delicate one that hemmed in the tulips, orchids, and roses she grew. She also replaced the path leading to the sea with more natural-looking stones that she handpicked, directing staff—irritated that steps Churchill had walked on did not even seem to be good enough for her—to plant grass between them to soften the way.[9]

Once, Kiki Moutsatsos, Onassis's assistant, asked her why she constantly tried to improve on her surroundings. "Are you that way in your New York home, too?" she asked.

"I suppose I am," Jackie replied. "But the truth is I love to decorate and change things. I want my houses to express my personality in everything I use there. There are so many things in this world that I cannot change, but when it comes to furniture and draperies and flowers . . . " [10]

On this day, Jackie couldn't help but think that all of the comfort and safety that Onassis, his island, and his money had provided were gone. Feeling overwhelmed, she had asked Moutsatsos to help.

"There is so much to do, Kiki," Jackie said resting in a chair. "I had not realized how much I had left to do until now."

"You don't have to do everything today," Moutstatsos told her. "After all you will come back often. All the people in Skorpios like you so much. They will be sad if you do not return often."

But Jackie knew that was not true. She knew that Christina did not want her there. So she stood up and got back to work. For hours she went through the house, tagging items that she wanted, remembering the shops where she bought an antique vase or candlestick, the moment she was surprised by a gift from Onassis, the conversations with her sisters-in-law about where to find the perfect rug.

Jackie and Moutstatsos walked to the yacht. The last item she tagged on board was a jade Buddha decorated with rubies. It was one of Onassis's prized possessions and although Christina initially objected to her taking it, she had relented. Jackie walked to the deck of the boat, looked out to the sea, and wept. Moutstatsos began to walk away, to give her privacy, when Jackie caught her.

"Would you mind, Kiki, if I told you this one little story?" she asked, choking back tears. "One day Aristo and I were sitting together outside the pink house and he was feeling very tender. 'Honey,' he said to me, 'the woman, you know, is like the world.'"

"Oh, really, Ari?" Jackie had answered him, bracing for a crude joke. "And how is that true?"

"'At twenty years, she is like Africa. Semi-explored. At thirty years, she is like India. Warm, mature, and mysterious. At forty, she is like America. Technically perfect. At fifty years, she is like Europe. All in ruins. At sixty years, she is like Siberia. Everyone knows where she is, but no one wants to go to her' . . . When he finished this little tale, I laughed and touched his mouth and said he was a philosopher. 'You must promise to tell me that tale every ten years,' I told him. And he agreed. Then I kissed him and I could tell that he felt very pleased with himself. His life. And with me. And now I cannot stop thinking about that day." [11]

Jackie returned to New York, where the newspaper headlines were agonizing for her. Stories about the attempted divorce lingered, forcing her to respond with a statement that went out over the wire: "I'll answer with something my husband [Onassis] often told me: 'Throughout the world people love fairy tales and especially those related to the lives of the rich. You must learn to understand this and accept it." [12] On top of that, gossips were sniping that she had been spending like mad as Onassis became more ill, forcing Nancy Tuckerman to say that Jackie had to buy many items for her new home in New Jersey. "Life must go on," Tuckerman said.[13] But the final indignity was a new book by Benjamin Bradlee—now, no longer a friend because of his disclosures—who had essentially transcribed his diary, including evenings with his wife at the White House with Jack and Jackie, for *Conversations with Kennedy*. The book's excerpts were splashed across *Newsweek*, *Playboy*, *Good Housekeeping*, and the *Washington Post*, where Bradlee has been executive editor since 1965.

> *We served as insulation tonight for a family squabble over finances at the White House. Jackie had just learned (remarkably enough) that her husband was giving his salary to charity and had told him earlier that day that she sure could use the money herself. A series of questions had evidently ensued, which led to a request for information from the President about the state of the family finances. He had the information in a letter which he had with him and which had him boiling . . . not so much mad, as amazed and indignant. The item that had him really bugged was "Department Stores—$40,000." No one had an explanation, much less Jackie. No furnishings for the White House, and as Jackie pointed out, "no sable coat, or any-thing." Kennedy announced that he had called in Carmine Bellino, an accounting expert for various Senate committees on deciphering the financial records of Mafiosi and a longtime Kennedy friend, to straighten out the family's finances. He said Bobby had recently called*

*in Bellino to straighten out Ethel's finances . . . Kennedy said he
could understand why running for the presidency was expensive. He
had spent and spent, he said—all of it capital. But "once you're in
here, this is a place where a fellow should at least break even, with all
the services provided."* [14]

It took more than a decade, but the myth of Camelot was
crumbling, like so much else around Jackie.

With Onassis's death behind her and spring in bloom, Jackie
was grateful to have another rite of passage to focus on: Caroline's high school graduation. Jackie dressed in understated
fashion with a spread-collar blouse beneath a double-breasted
trench with wide lapels, a couple of long thick chains weigh-
ing around her neck. She settled into her folding chair on the
lawn, thirteen rows back from the stage. Seated beside her were
Ted and his mother, Rose Kennedy, wearing pearls and a wide-
brimmed hat on this sunny day, June 5, 1975. Lee was there,
too, with their mother, Janet. And so was John Jr., whose boarding school adventures Jackie had decided to delay so she could
keep an eye on him a little longer. The extended family was
there to celebrate Caroline's graduation and to support Jackie.

The strangers around them buzzed with constrained excitement of seeing their famous faces, checking out their clothes
and those unmistakable teeth, and noting sadly that one Kennedy was even more conspicuous in his absence. They tried

hard not to stare. This was Massachusetts after all, and Ted was their senator. But some did search for clues on Jackie's face about whether she was upset by the latest news: half of Onassis's fortune would be allocated to a charity set up in his son's name. Christina had chosen this day to make the news public.

Caroline never enjoyed the spotlight that had surrounded her most of her seventeen years. And out of respect for her and her classmates, the school had set up a barricade to keep the media penned in. They remained there, two photographers scuffling with a local police officer, as Caroline approached the stage to receive her diploma. But she was embarrassed to be in

June 5, 1975. Nancy Tuckerman blocks a UPI photographer at Caroline's graduation from Concord Academy. Senator Edward M. Kennedy is on the left. *(Bettman/CORBIS)*

June 5, 1975. Caroline's graduation, with her mother, grandmothers, brother, and uncle Ted. *(Bettman/CORBIS)*

front of so many, the star of the day, and she rolled her eyes as she accepted her scroll.

Jackie beamed from her seat. She also saw that despite the setting's traditional backdrop, with ancient trees and white clapboard buildings, change was all around her. The school, which had been strict and all girls, had recently loosened the rules and allowed boys to enroll. Caroline, chewing gum and wearing a white lace dress with peasant sleeves and a hem that skimmed the grass, seemed to be commencing into a world very different from the one Jackie had faced when she graduated from Miss Porter's.

During the recessional, the graduates strolled down the

center aisle in twos. Jackie leaned out, whispering to Caroline, words no one else heard. When the ceremony was over, the family posed for a few snapshots, which the news photographers also caught. And Jackie presented her daughter with a poignant gift—a tool to see life in new ways, a tool that had enabled Jackie's first job. It was a camera.[15]

Two days later, reality again crashed the celebration. One of Onassis's aides, Stelios Papadimitriou, released to the press his boss's eighteen-page handwritten will, drafted on the millionaire's private jet as it flew from Acapulco to New York in January 1974. The details were on the front page of the *Washington Post*, and spread beneath a splashy headline in the *Los Angeles Times*. The stories explained that Onassis had left the bulk of his estate to his daughter, Christina, and that Jackie would receive $250,000 a year, including $25,000 for each of her children.[16] Christina would also own 75 percent of his yacht and Skorpios, with Jackie owning the other 25 percent of each.

"If the two women do not want Skorpios," he wrote, "it should first be offered as a resort for the head of the state. If again turned down, it should be given to Olympic Airways as a holiday resort for the company's employees."

Onassis signed his will, "With my last kiss, Daddy."[17]

CHAPTER SIX

The Seeker

I f 1963 was a horrific year, then 1975 was a close second. After months of sadness, anger, uncertainty, backbiting, and press scrutiny, Jackie sought comfort in her old friend Tish Baldrige. After her stint as White House social secretary in the Kennedy administration, Baldrige had stayed in Washington, started a family, and launched an eponymous public relations firm with clients such as Cartier, Tiffany, and Elizabeth Arden. Baldrige had spoken with Jackie on a few occasions since Onassis had died about three months earlier and had heard the sadness in Jackie's voice. She had also read the headlines about Grand Central, the divorce threat, the estate battle. They needed to catch up in person. As always, Baldrige executed the plan.

Naturally, Baldrige knew just the place to have an important lunch with Jackie—the Sulgrave Club, in Dupont Circle. And there she waited, at a corner table, where they would meet in quiet and safety in a city full of journalists and power lunchers. And while it was not Baldrige's intent, the restaurant, a women's club, was also a poetic choice for the conversation the two were about to have. The club was part of what had once been a grand home on Massachusetts Avenue owned in the early 1900s by a wealthy couple, Herbert and Martha Wadsworth. Martha Wadsworth, like an earlier version of Jackie, had been an exceptional horsewoman, a prolific photographer, a presence on the social scene, and had more than an eye for architecture, designing, and furnishing her Beaux-Arts style house, built of light-yellow Roman brick and cream-colored, molded terra-cotta.[1]

Sitting there alone before her famous friend arrived, Baldrige remembered the various aspects of Jackie's life—many of them lived in public—that had shaped her, and led her to this crucible of middle age, with no husband, no career, no real agenda beyond her newfound preservation work. Jackie had decided to keep John in school in New York, at Collegiate, before releasing him to boarding school. Come September, Caroline would be gone, studying in London, and Jackie would be much more alone. And then what? *What was she going to do with the rest of her life?* The point of the lunch was clear, at least to Baldrige. Jackie needed to find meaningful employment, both to engage and distract her.

Although the two of them had precisely the same

education—Miss Porter's and Vassar, followed by time in Paris, the outcomes so far had been different. Baldrige, tall, forthright, and tireless, had delayed starting a family during her around-the-clock White House career, despite what she was taught at Miss Porter's. Jackie, even without a career, was always hungry for knowledge and found it instead in her social interactions, soaking up history at the opening of the races at Longchamps, sitting in the Bibliotheque National, walking the ruins on an island. Jackie never wanted to be trapped in that life—but she wasn't going to be trapped at work, either. And in reality, she never really needed to be.

Jackie had been astounded after graduation when Baldrige had chosen a career, something Tish believed was necessary for happiness. Jackie had respected her friend's decision—but then lured her away from a position as a public relations executive in Milan by asking her to work in the White House, where Baldrige enjoyed having lunch in the mess hall so she could argue with men. Jackie respected her friend, but was "exhausted" by her.[2] When Baldrige left her White House job in 1963, JFK told her she was the most "emotional" woman he had ever met.[3] Fine if Tish wanted a job, but "working" was not for Jackie.

By 1975, the world had changed significantly. Burning bras was no longer new. *The Mary Tyler Moore Show,* one of the first on TV to portray an independent career woman (Mary was a producer at a television news station), was already in its fifth season, and had just won an Emmy for Best Comedy Series a few weeks before Jackie and Tish met for lunch. But Jackie still belonged to a different generation and social class in which ladies of good families apologized for being at work—if they worked at all. Jackie had always been protected by men. But now she had a daughter about to launch on her own trajectory. Perhaps Jackie thought that Caroline would have to be the one trying to figure out this strange new world, this thing called feminism, where women, even those who did not have to, pursued a career—and not just for the money, but for their own self-worth.

Baldrige, her napkin in her lap as she waited for Jackie to arrive at the Sulgrave Club, continued an internal dialogue to hash through her friend's options.[4] The corporate world was definitely not for her. Jackie was not the kind of person who would punch a clock at a specific hour every day. But maybe Jackie would like a job in the nonprofit sector? Something where you could keep your own hours? At the time, Jackie was being deluged with requests from people asking to lend her name to committees, especially ones involved in preservation, as well as from endorsements, particularly in fashion. To Jackie, most of those requests were about what a cause could get out of her, rather than what she could get out of it.

Years before, in 1964, Dorothy Schiff, the longtime owner and publisher of the *New York Post*, had met with Jackie in Manhattan. It was one week after the release of the Warren Report, which declared that Lee Harvey Oswald had acted alone in the assassination. Jackie was very emotional with Schiff, her eyes brimming with tears when she explained that she had forgotten to cancel her newspaper and magazine subscriptions that week and had been forced to see the coverage of the report when the shooting was still so fresh.

"There is only one thing to do," Schiff told her. "And that is to find a substitute in work that is all-absorbing. It will never be the same thing, but you can lose yourself that way."

Jackie told her that she knew that was true and would like to do it.

"I don't want to be Ambassador to France or Mexico," she told Schiff. "President Johnson said I could have anything I wanted. I would like to work for somebody, but the list is . . . One is expecting someone to come home every weekend, but no one . . ."

Schiff was sympathetic and admitted that a job was a poor replacement for the void in her life.

"You know, you are the most famous and admired woman in the world," Schiff said. "It is quite a responsibility."

Being a political wife, that had been her job, a job that left her tired and hoarse at the end of the day. After a pause in her conversation with Schiff, her mind wandered back to the White House.

"All that furniture . . ."

Before she left, Schiff offered Jackie a job as a columnist.

"You could just write about things you go to and anything you like," said Schiff, who had been a columnist herself.

"Oh, I can't write," Jackie said, reflexively reverting to her old-fashioned demure ways. But she also huffed that she had received lots of requests from magazines to write about what one might expect—gracious living or fashion—not about the space race or civil rights or global affairs. After all, she said, her voice growing indignant, "I am interested in the same things Jack was interested in!"[5]

As Jackie finally entered the room at the Sulgrave Club—eleven years after that conversation with Schiff—Baldrige was struck by how impeccably dressed her friend was and how depressed she looked and sounded. Even her voice was "drooping." After settling in and ordering lunch, Baldrige was blunt, as old friends can be.

"You're so smart and so bright and you've hidden all that under a bushel," Baldrige said. "It's time to step out with it. Go to work and get a job."

"Who, me—work?" Jackie asked. "And do what?"

They discussed foundation work but that didn't seem right.

"Well, you care about publishing, you've been doing things, advising people on their books, you should get a job as a publisher."[6]

Publishing was not the nonprofit world, but it was close. Baldrige, who was in the process of completing a manuscript called *Juggling*, about balancing work, marriage, and motherhood, suggested her publisher, Viking Press.

"Look," Baldrige encouraged, "you know Tommy Guinzburg. Why don't you talk to him?"

Thomas Henry Guinzburg was president of Viking, the distinguished New York publishing house. He had known Jackie's stepbrother in college. They knew each other from the days of Lee's marriage to Canfield. And they inhabited similar New York social circles. Viking had published some heady work: D. H. Lawrence, Steinbeck, and Kerouac, whose novel *On the Road* Jackie had read while on the presidential campaign. Viking was still a small publisher, and it had a niche in art books, which Jackie was always collecting. She made no promises to Baldrige about Viking, but Jackie's sad eyes briefly sparkled at the idea of looking for work. Before the lunch ended—it was a quick fifty minutes as they both had other obligations—Baldrige could see that Jackie was motivated to change her life, to be her own person. Jackie wasn't a feminist. In fact, she would have balked at the term. But whether she knew it or not, she was following a feminist path—as well as her heart, and her talent.

Jackie was always reading—Proust on the lawn in Hyannis Port, de Gaulle's memoirs in French at home in the White House, or Greek poetry on the *Christina*.[7] She had majored in French literature. She had been there for the birth of *Profiles in Courage*. Jack did not give her candy or flowers. He gave her books, serious ones at that, such as *The Raven* and *Pilgrim's Way*.[8]

She had been related to a publisher. She was related to authors (Gore Vidal and Louis Auchincloss) and she surrounded herself with other writers—inviting French novelist and minister of cultural affairs André Malraux to 1600 Pennsylvania

Avenue, George Plimpton to parties at Hammersmith Farm, and Truman Capote, before their relationship cooled, to 1040 Fifth. She had always dreamed of writing a novel,[9] and had produced a couple of books of her own. Her first was *The White House: An Historic Guide,* for which Jackie chose every item, read every word, looked at every layout, and chose every typeface. The book went on sale to the public for a dollar apiece on July 4, 1962. Within six months, 350,000 copies were sold. The first book was presented to the Kennedys on June 28, 1962. As they walked out of the Fish Room in the West Wing, Jackie said to J. B. West, the usher, "Now J. B., I want it understood that everyone has to pay [the cover price of] $1, even Ethel." Now in its twenty-second edition, it still funds White House museum work.[10] The other was *One Special Summer,* the scrapbook (that Lee found while working on her own memoirs) that had just been published in 1974.

Jackie loved words, stories, poems, and pictures, and how they fit together. She devoured not only books but also magazines, such as *Paris Match,* a sort of French version of *Life.* In addition to her love of reading, she also possessed two other elements that could make her a fine editor. First, she had a love for writing. Despite what she told Schiff, she *could* write and it was a talent that she kept mostly private.

She could also pack a punch with short essays, such as one she submitted to *Look* magazine on the one-year anniversary of the assassination. "Now I think that I should have known that he was magic all along," she wrote. "I did know it—but I should have guessed it could not last. I should have known that it was asking too much to dream that I might have grown old with him and see our children grow up together. So now he is a legend when he would have preferred to be a man . . . His high noon kept all the freshness of the morning—and he died then, never knowing disillusionment. 'He has gone/ . . . Among the radiant, ever venturing on,/ Somewhere, with morning, as such spirits will.' " The final quote she pulled from John Masefield's "On the Finish of the Sailing Ship Race." [11]

The second talent that could make her adept as a conceptual editor was her ability to stagecraft, knowing how to pull together characters, backdrops, dialogue, and stay true to a theme. She had accomplished this with so many elements of her life—grand funerals, her fashion image, even the Camelot myth that she had seemingly made up on the spot during an interview with *Life* journalist Theodore White a week after JFK was shot.

Beyond all that, Jackie had had a parade of intense book experiences. For more than a decade after the assassination, memoirs exposing almost every aspect of her life were written by those closest to her: the cook, who had disclosed that Jackie had dieted off twenty-five pounds; the nanny, who had broken the news to Caroline that her father was dead; her husband's longtime secretary, who complained about not getting a raise; and by journalists who had been reverent during the presidency but were crass—at least in Jackie's eyes—in their later books.

———

One of these men had been Jim Bishop, who had written *The Day Lincoln Was Shot*, detailing the assassination minute by minute. The book was a massive success when it was published in 1955, and it was later made into a movie. JFK was enamored with the idea of what Bishop could do for his legacy, and had given the writer complete access to the White House, resulting in *A Day in the Life of President Kennedy*. Kennedy was dead before the book was done. But Jackie had resented the author's presence in her life and did not think Bishop, who had dropped out of school in the eighth grade, was a good writer. In the days after Dallas, Bishop, a syndicated columnist, announced that he was going to write a new book, *The Day Kennedy Was Shot*, another moment-by-moment account that was published in 1968. Jackie, seeking revenge and needing to assert some control over a spiraling situation, tried to preempt him by handpicking her own writer, to whom she would divulge everything, and whose draft of history she would trust.[12]

She asked Theodore White. He said no. She asked Walter Lord, who wrote *A Night to Remember*, a harrowing account of the *Titanic* sinking. He, too, said no.

Next on her list was Massachusetts native William Manchester, a tall, pipe-smoking Wesleyan University fellow who had received a Purple Heart in Okinawa as a marine. After the war, he had been a *Baltimore Sun* reporter and then he became an author, writing biographies of H. L. Mencken, the Rockefellers, and JFK, for which he, too, had had White House access. His glowing *Portrait of a President: John F. Kennedy in Profile* was published in 1962.

"I'd see Jack at the end of his last appointment for the day. We'd have a daiquiri and sit on the Truman balcony," Manchester would say later.

Jackie had read every glowing word of Manchester's *Portrait* and loved it. On February 5, 1964, he was in his office in the Wesleyan library when the phone rang. It was Pierre Salinger, JFK's former press secretary, asking him to write an authorized account of the assassination.

"How can I say no to Mrs. Kennedy?" Manchester asked his secretary, who was sitting right there.

"You can't," she said.

A few weeks later, Manchester, his literary agent Don Congdon, and Harper & Row's Evan Thomas (he had edited *Profiles in Courage* and RFK's *The Enemy Within*) met with Bobby, still attorney general, in his Washington office. To avoid the appearance that anyone was making money off of Jack's death, they capped Harper's profits and gave Manchester a $40,000 advance, agreeing that any additional proceeds would go to the JFK Library. Before they left, Robert produced a memo saying, among other things, that the book would not be published for five years, to give everyone enough time to heal, and that "the final text shall not be published unless and until approved" by him and Jackie.

Manchester went to work, leaving his wife and three kids in

Connecticut to finish out the school year before they could join him in an inexpensive apartment in DC. His first of two long interviews with Jackie occurred in April 1964, at her house in Georgetown. She was wearing a black jersey and yellow stretch pants.

"She was beaming at me," Manchester would remember. "And I thought how, at age thirty-four, with her camellia beauty, she might have been taken for a woman in her mid-twenties. My first impression, and it never changed—was that I was in the presence of a very great tragic actress."

They sat. Manchester put his dictionary-size Wollensak tape recorder where she would not be reminded of its presence. They, too, drank daiquiris—she had too many—and over the course of several hours, she conjured wrenching, minute details of what happened in the Fort Worth hotel room on her and Jack's final night together, what bloody hell had become of the backseat of the Lincoln the next day, and what the scene looked like in Trauma Room No. 1 at Parkland Hospital.

For the next two years Manchester would work long days, seven days a week, interview a thousand people, walk the sixth floor of the Texas School Book Depository, and watch the Zapruder film nearly one hundred times. He spoke with virtually everyone who had seen or heard anything between November 21, 1963, and the burial at Arlington. The only people who refused to speak with him were the Johnsons. The depressing subject matter, combined with stress and exhaustion, pushed him to the brink of a breakdown; he even called his wife, Julia, "Jacqueline." Eventually, he was hospitalized. But within two weeks, Manchester was back at the typewriter. When he was done, the final manuscript was 1,201 pages.[13]

Thomas, his editor, was ecstatic, believing it was the finest book he had read in twenty years. Bobby had agreed to an earlier publication date so as not to conflict with the election year of 1968, but he passed on reading it, not wanting to dredge up more sadness. Jackie did the same. The review fell to a handful of Kennedy aides, who thought the manuscript made the Johnsons look like boors, and Manchester divulged too many details that were private. They gave edits to Thomas. Manchester, desperate to know what was happening, received a telegram from Bobby on July 29, 1966, saying:

WHILE I HAVE NOT READ WILLIAM MANCHESTER'S ACCOUNT OF THE DEATH OF PRESIDENT KENNEDY . . . MEMBERS OF THE KENNEDY FAMILY WILL PLACE NO OBSTACLE IN THE WAY OF PUBLICATION OF HIS WORK.

With that, Manchester's agent approached several magazines to publish an advance serialization. *Look* won the bid, offering a then record $665,000. But Jackie was furious that anyone should make that kind of money off the story. She asked Pamela Turnure, Baldrige's replacement as White House secretary, to read the manuscript. There was a great deal of emotional exposure for Jackie, Turnure said. Manchester even disclosed that Jackie smoked—supposedly a well-kept secret. And there was too much information about the children.

For months, Jackie battled Manchester and his team privately. She threatened to ruin Thomas. Ultimately, she filed an injunction against Harper and the publisher of *Look*—a move that blew the lid off the long-simmering feud. The drama was front-page news across the country. JFK BOOK BATTLE: MRS. KENNEDY LEAVES MEETING WITH *LOOK* MAGAZINE IN TEARS, one report blared. Manchester defended himself on *Meet the Press*. The situation had become, in the words of *Time* magazine, "the biggest brouhaha over a book that the nation has ever known."[14]

In the end, Jackie, who had always been astute at public relations, lost on many levels. Some of the Kennedys' edits were made. But *Look* published its serialization. And by fighting with Manchester, she was drawing more attention to his work. Jackie, despite having the world's sympathy after the assassination, looked petulant and naive, saying, "I thought that it would be bound in black and put away on dark library shelves." The book, which sold 600,000 copies within the first two months, generated more than a $1 million in royalties—all of which went to the JFK Library.[15]

Eventually, Jackie sat down in her apartment to read the book. She stayed up through the night and when she was done, she had only one word to describe it: "Fascinating."[16]

———

Not long after that lunch with Baldrige, Jackie was back in New York and on a mission to find work in publishing. Harper & Row was not an option, not after the Manchester battle. However, her first call was not to Guinzburg, as her friend had suggested, perhaps because the "ask" seemed too easy at a time when she was looking to be challenged. Rather, she reached out to another acquaintance, Jason Epstein, the editorial director at Random House, which in addition to publishing Jim Bishop's book had also published Vladimir Nabokov, Norman Mailer, Arthur Miller, and Jackie's stepbrother Gore Vidal. Epstein, a classic New York intellectual and the founder of the *New York Review of Books*, knew Jackie well. They had a lot of friends in common. He was known to be shrewd and tough. His response might be more honest, making Jackie feel more certain of herself.

She invited him to lunch at the famed Lutèce, a three-star restaurant she knew he would like because the French food was the best in the city and it was around the corner from his office at Third Avenue and Fiftieth Street. Of course, Epstein said yes to meeting with her there a week later. But as he approached the door of Lutèce, he braced himself. Jackie's "gasping" and "breathless" manner of speech always unnerved him. He also remembered what his friend, the journalist Pete Hamill, had said: that taking Jackie out was like "taking King Kong to the beach."

They met upstairs at the restaurant, in a private room. Epstein, with his editor's eye for detail, noted that she was wearing pink, one of her favorite colors, and one that looked very nice on her. They ordered the shad roe, a culinary symbol of the rebirth of spring, prepared in sorrel sauce. And then she said, "I'm looking for a job."

Epstein was surprised not only to hear that she wanted a career in publishing but also that he was her first stop on the search. He knew she was smart. He knew she would be a good colleague and be fun to have around, that she had connections with lots of people and anyone would take her call. She had access and brains—and was a regular at all the best restaurants in town—which counted for a lot in the book business. He told her all of this.

But publishing was a very competitive industry. Young people arrived straight out of college to work their way in however possible, fetching coffee, securing theater tickets, answering the phones, filing, responding to unsolicited manuscripts—anything to get their foot in the door. It would take years of grooming before they could be rewarded with an editing position. Epstein had three or four such eager and loyal employees waiting for the next opening. How could Jackie cut the line? It would be like jumping the list at an exclusive country club.

He'd have to create a position, he told her. He had all of these young people working to advance.

Jackie, whose instincts and social graces were perfection, backed off immediately and changed the subject before he could even say that he'd like to discuss it with his colleagues. They chatted pleasantly for another hour. She left half the food on the plate—and skipped dessert. They walked out together and down a half block to the Random House office, saying good-bye on the sidewalk. Epstein, back at his desk, was just beginning to realize the enormous mistake he had made—one for which he would always be sorry.[17]

Jackie was mortified. There was no way she was going to repeat the Epstein lunch debacle. But she needed to carry on with her quest. Instead of cold-calling Guinzburg, she asked Baldrige to do it for her, as if a friend were arranging a date in junior high school. Except it was for lunch at Le Périgord, yet another fine French restaurant.

Guinzburg was surprised to hear Baldrige's Julia Child–like voice asking him if he would meet with Jackie to discuss the possibility of employment. But the substance of her request was not without reason. He and Jackie had known each other for close to twenty years. He, too, knew she was smart. But more than that, publishing at that time was as much about the people you knew as what you knew. Not only did Jackie know some of the world's most intriguing people, but she could also get anyone to do anything. From Jackie's perspective, the house would be a good fit because it was informal and small, making it a great place to learn. Viking also had a division called Studio Books, which published high-quality art and photography by people she knew well: Jacques Lowe, who had chronicled the 1960 presidential campaign; Richard Avedon, who had photographed her, Jack, and the kids in Palm Beach; and Peter Beard, a guest on Skorpios and Lee's occasional boyfriend. It had also published books on topics associated with Jackie: Anne Lincoln's *The Kennedy White House Parties* (1967) and John Sweeney's *The Treasure House of Early American Rooms* (1963).

Guinzburg was a tall, smart man with big hands, a big smile, and literary chops. His father, Harold, had founded Viking in 1925, the year before Tom was born. As a boy, Tom Guinzburg had read children's book manuscripts for his father and made recommendations about which ones he thought should be published. After graduating from Hotchkiss, he enlisted in the marines during World War II, where, in addition to learning the importance of integrity, he received a Purple Heart at Iwo Jima. After the war, he was an English major at Yale, ran the paper there, and roomed with a young man named William F. Buckley. But as with many others interested in literature at the time, Paris beckoned for Guinzburg. And it was there that with a few hundred dollars in seed money he founded the *Paris Review* with four eager young Americans, including his other college roommate, Peter Matthiessen, and George Plimpton, who was just launching a career as an experiential journalist. Guinzburg's French was adequate enough for him to get around the city at night, but his time running a newspaper in

New Haven was hardly enough to make him a success as managing editor of this new magazine, in his own estimation. "I was a complete failure at the *Paris Review*," he said years later.[18] So in June 1953, he returned home, to Viking. During those first years back in New York, he ran with the city's literati, was there in 1960 when Norman Mailer stabbed his wife, and had John Steinbeck as the best man at his second wedding. When his friend Jackie ascended to First Lady, he sent books to the White House—including Ludwig Bemelmans's children's classic, *Madeline*. Jackie loved the story of the French orphan girl so much she corresponded with the author and even considered writing a children's book with him. Bemelmans sent her a blank journal to encourage her to record her experiences in the White House but he died in 1962 before they could collaborate.[19] In addition to *Madeline,* Guinzburg also sent Jackie the art books she cherished. In return, she'd send him little notes scrawled with a special pen on a card.

After the assassination, when Jackie had moved back to Manhattan and craved evenings out that were interesting rather than just simply fashionable, she'd go to Elaine's, a club that Guinzburg, Plimpton, and their intellectual friends had made popular with a crowd that would later include Andy Warhol.

Guinzburg had assumed the helm of the Viking ship, which now faced financial difficulties. He ran the operation from an opulent office, which had a Viking helmet on the windowsill, and a dartboard on the wall containing pictures of agents and reviewers who annoyed him.[20] He knew what made a good editor; that's all he hired. But he also understood the importance of notoriety, a less subtle way to encourage writers and agents to send their best work to the house, and for readers to buy books. Jackie would be a public relations boon for Viking. He recognized that right away. But still, this was her idea, not his.

They met at Le Périgord, which, because it was not far from the United Nations, was a draw for diplomats and politicians. By the end of their meal, they agreed in principal that she would work at Viking. But they still needed to settle some important details, and made a date to meet at her apartment at 1040 Fifth.

There, he made his way past the doorman, up the elevator that opened to her apartment, and by the domestic help into the sanctuary of Jackie's home. She greeted him warmly and brought him into the living room. He peered out French doors that offered a magnificent view of the Metropolitan Museum of Art and its new enclosure, which would house the Temple of Dendur, a Cleopatra-era monument about eighty-two feet long that had once stood on the banks of the Nile. The temple was sent to America in appreciation of the $12 million in federal funds that Jackie had convinced JFK to offer Egypt for saving temples that were at risk of flooding when the Aswan Dam was built.[21] Now it was being reconstructed stone block by stone block on an island—Manhattan—within Jackie's daily view. That something so monumental and literally set in stone could have a new life seemed symbolic at that moment in 1975. And Jackie made a mental note to bring Caroline for a private tour of the project when she graduated in a few weeks. The reconstruction work was almost done, and it was marvelous to see.[22]

She and Guinzburg had barely begun to talk when the phone rang, a call Jackie had to take. Just then, Caroline bounded in and plunked down her bag. With her light brown waves, all one length just past her shoulders and parted in the middle, Caroline looked the part of the irreverent teenager.

Caroline spied Guinzburg sitting alone and approached him.

"Is my mom gonna go work for you?" she asked.

"Yeah, I think so," he said.

Caroline grimaced, as if she had just smelled something rotten. It was the face of a typical daughter who did not think her mother was capable of doing anything, let alone getting a job. He chuckled. Jackie returned to the room and Caroline retreated elsewhere in the apartment.

The two settled in to talk. This was not an interview. In his mind, she already had the job. It was just the details that needed to be finalized.

"What title do you want?" he asked her. "It might be hard to throw you in as an editor."

"How about associate editor? I kind of like that."

But associate editor would have meant that she would have line-editing responsibilities—something for which she had no experience. They agreed she should start as a consulting editor, which meant all she really had to do was acquire books, spot talent, and bring ideas to the table. She would have Mondays off for the hairdresser, and Fridays off for horse riding at her new country home in New Jersey. There might be other days not in the office because she would be in the library.

Salary?

"I don't care about money," she told him. "This is not about that."

He explained that market pay was about $10,000 a year. The sum was fine with Jackie, but they both knew that she could spend that entire year's salary in one fitting at Valentino.

They agreed she'd start her job after Labor Day. Publishing was notoriously slow in the summer, with the industry fleeing the city in August. And besides, Jackie had a few other important milestones that would consume the season.

CHAPTER SEVEN

The
Hot Prospect

Jackie could have been forgiven if she never wanted to step foot in Greece again, but she mustered her strength and with her kids planned one last trip to Skorpios for July, when she would turn forty-six, to say a proper good-bye, round up what remained of their belongings, and pack in the memories.

Jackie also invited her New York friend Karl Katz, as well as *Paris Review* editor Clem Wood and his wife.[1] Onassis's sister Artemis would also be joining them.

But this would not be the relaxing vacation any of them hoped for. Jackie, for one, felt the doors to the past slamming

July 14, 1975. Saying good-bye to Skorpios. *(Anastasselis Polydoros/Gamma-Rapho via Getty Images)*

shut all around her. Her parents had just told her that Hammersmith Farm, the childhood home that she loved and the place that had hosted her first wedding reception, was finally sold after four years on the market in a deal that was not yet public.[2] And Tuckerman—her right arm for so many years—

would be starting a new job in publishing as the assistant to Doubleday's publisher, Sam Vaughan, working in the publicity and promotion department, creating special events for authors. That news was also still a secret.[3]

Then, shortly after they landed on the tiny island, Jackie learned of more surprising news. Christina was going to marry Alexander Andreades—the son of a wealthy industrialist whose grandfather had been Greece's prime minister. Christina had only known him for a month and had become engaged the week before.[4]

Meanwhile, despite front-page headlines implying that Jackie had been relatively cut off from Onassis's vast fortune, few people knew that Christina and her stepmother were privately negotiating a settlement in the $20 million range. Once that deal was done, they never had to speak to each other again. For now, Jackie was trying to keep up appearances. Christina, under pressure from her aunt Artemis, invited Jackie to attend her wedding.[5] Regardless of the acrimony between them and the media circus that would likely ensue, Jackie and her son flew from Skorpios to Athens for the ceremony, held at a tiny, sweltering church surrounded by cypress and olive trees in Glyfada.[6]

About a hundred people crammed the street outside the chapel trying to catch a glimpse of this unlikely family: the troubled heiress, America's queen, and the handsome, dark-haired teenager. Old ladies dressed in black and mothers pushing baby carriages jockeyed for position along with the paparazzi. Police were there attempting to maintain order and not succeeding as the bystanders and photographers rushed the first limousine, this one carrying the groom. When he emerged from a car wearing a blue suit with red pinstripes and holding a cigarette in its plastic holder, the crowd applauded him. He seemed surprised.

Jackie, John, and Christina arrived forty-five minutes late. When Jackie stepped out of the limousine, the crowd surged toward her, leaving plenty of room for the bride and her stepbrother to climb out of the car. Christina wore an off-white lay-

July 22, 1975. Bride Christina Onassis Andreadis and her groom, Alexander Andreadis (right), chat with the groom's father, Stratis Andreadis, during the garden party following the couple's wedding in Athens. *(Bettman/CORBIS)*

ered gown with a purple sash and a gold cross around her neck. She made her way inside, was married in a Greek Orthodox ceremony, and emerged once again confronted by the gawkers, this time shouting their wishes of *"Na zisete!"* Long life to you.[7]

John complained about the temperature. "Gosh, it was hot in there," he said.[8]

Jackie was more sophisticated in her public remarks, her words perhaps reflecting her hopes for herself.

"I'm so happy for that girl," she said. "There is a lot of happiness ahead for her after a great deal of sadness."[9]

But it was not to be. Almost immediately, Christina was completely alone again. The groom, in the army, had to return to his barracks without a honeymoon. Their marriage lasted only fourteen months. Then, in 1978, Christina married a one-eyed Russian, Sergei Kauzov, who was a former Soviet shipping executive and a suspected KGB agent. Their relationship ended within sixteen months. Christina, adrift, battling weight that exceeded two hundred pounds on her five-foot-five-inch frame, and trying to improve her looks with hair dye or plastic surgery, married for the fourth and final time in 1984 to French businessman Thierry Roussel, her crush as a teenager. They had a daughter, Athina, before divorcing in 1987 after he left her for another woman. A year later, while visiting friends in Buenos Aires, where her father first sought to make a fortune, Christina followed her family's tragic path as she was visiting friends: The official cause of death was pulmonary edema, or fluid in the lungs, perhaps caused by a heart attack. But she had sleeping pills by her side in her room, where she was found in the tub, in a few inches of water.[10] Christina, three weeks shy of her thirty-eighth birthday, was buried on Skorpios near her father and brother. Jackie did not attend the funeral.[11]

Jackie, her friends, and family—after a languid good-bye to Skorpios, the yacht, the Ionian Sea, and whatever luxury, peace, and privacy they had been afforded over the last seven years— were headed home, back to the noisy streets of New York. Shortly after she landed in the sweltering city Jackie was struck by yet another hard reality. Skorpios had not been the completely private retreat she thought. Perhaps it never was.

Hustler magazine's cover that month, August 1975, featured a woman's round, white, naked rear, set off by an ink-black backdrop and the words:

EXCLUSIVE
JACQUELINE
KENNEDY
ONASSIS
NUDE

There were no exclamation points necessary. *Hustler* publisher Larry Flynt had bought the photos from a paparazzo, who had taken the shots of Jackie from a distance on the water off Skorpios four years earlier. She eventually knew the shots had been taken, but Onassis had refused to sue the photographer because he was too "cheap" to make it worthy.[12] Five full-page color photographs showed Jackie totally naked, her wet hair pushed back from her face. Two were frontal shots, with her standing, holding a blue beach towel beside her. Two others showed her walking away, but oblivious she was being watched. Another had her bending over. One million magazines, which included a nude poster of her, flew off the newsstands in just a few days. If there was any solace in being so exposed, it was this: she may have been in her forties, but she had the slim, toned body of a woman half her age.

As it does every August, New York's center of gravity shifts east, to Long Island. And Andy Warhol's oceanfront compound in Montauk was a special draw for celebrities. He had rented the property, known as the Church Estate, a cluster of bleached-out cottages, to Lee Radziwill beginning in 1972. This summer, he had kicked off the season by inviting the Rolling Stones to come and stay, to practice "Angie" and "It's Only Rock 'n Roll" for "The Americas Tour." They blared their music beyond the bluffs and then took off. The estate, called Eoönen, or dawn, was located—conveniently for Lee—next door to the artist Peter Beard, whose place overlooked the very tip of Long Island. Beard, a handsome Yale graduate, spent time on Skorpios with the sisters and had been working on a book called *Longing for Darkness* about meeting *Out of Africa* author Isak Dinesen.

When Random House had declined to publish the manuscript Jackie asked him what she could do to help. "Have a dance with Africans around a campfire in Newport?" [13] Instead, she wrote the afterword for the book, giving it an extra boost when it was finally published that summer:

What an extraordinary surprise and gift it was, when Peter Beard first showed me the fables and drawings of Isak Dinesen's beloved Kamante. I had not known he was still alive. To hold his drawings was like touching a talisman that took you back to a world you thought had disappeared forever.

Maybe I was so affected because Out of Africa *has always meant more to me than any other book. But then I watched my children respond to the fables with the freshness of young minds. My son started to make African drawings, some of which he asked Peter Beard to send to Kamante for him . . .*

Peter Beard reveals the immediacy her philosophy can have for the young people of today—who are so passionately idealistic, so ready to be martyrs. This book can help them; show them that they had allies in an earlier time, who knew that courage was endurance as well as abandon . . .

How contemporary Isak Dinesen is; her prescience of how man would destroy his environment, her belief that his only hope was to get in tune with it again. It seems to me that so many of the movements of today, ecology, anti-materialism, communal living— they were all in Out of Africa.

She was one of the first white people to feel that "black is beautiful." She was the first to see how "all the dark forces of time, evolution, nature" were being disrupted in Africa. Cecil Rhodes saying "teach the native to want" so quickly became Galbraith's "Affluent Society."

One of my favorite passages in Out of Africa is where Isak Dinesen asks: "If I know a song of Africa, of the giraffe and the African new moon lying on her back, of the ploughs in the fields and the sweaty faces of the coffee pickers, does Africa know a song of me? Would the air over the plain quiver with a color that I had on, or the children invent a game in which my name was, or the full moon throw a shadow over the gravel of the drive that was like me, or would the eagles of the Ngong Hills look out for me?"

This book is the echo she longed for. Yes, Africa does have a song for her. It is Peter Beard and Kamante who have made it for her.

Kamante's drawings and Peter Beard's photographs share a purity—of a wild animal looking at the camera with free and vulnerable eyes.

This book is a work of love—of a love that a young man, young enough to be her grandson, was struck with when he first read Out of Africa. The book changed his life. He went in search of that Africa she knew. He saves its memories, her memories, for us.

Before it is too late?

Now, here they were, in Montauk, celebrating Beard's success and marveling over the fact that Jackie's body was a major spread in *Hustler*. There was only one thing to do with the centerfold. She pulled it out and signed it for Warhol:

> *For Andy, with enduring affection,*
> *Jackie Montauk*

Leaving the beach behind for the city, Jackie wanted to check out a new Broadway production called *Chicago*. She went to the show with an old friend, the diamond merchant Maurice Tempelsman. He had first met her in the 1950s, when he had arranged a meeting for then senator Kennedy to discuss business interests in South Africa. During her White House years, Jackie had made frequent trips to New York, attending the theater with UN ambassador Adlai Stevenson, who had been Tempelsman's lawyer. Sometimes Tempelsman would tag along with them for dinner.

This time, it was just the two of them. But hardly anyone paid any attention. In many ways, Tempelsman was like many of Jackie's escorts, who fell into one of three categories: gay, married, or old. Tempelsman could appear a bit frumpy, but was merely middle-aged, born the same year as Jackie into a Yiddish-speaking Orthodox Jewish family in Belgium. He was definitely not gay. But he was married—with three kids.[14] That important fact aside, Jackie enjoyed him. Having fled Europe to America with his parents during World War II, he was fluent in French. He was also wise about finance and politics. He had joined his father's diamond business as a teenager, and now he was brokering deals directly with entire African governments. While Jackie was grappling with Onassis's declining health earlier in the year, Tempelsman was in Zaire (the former Belgian Congo), the biggest producer of diamonds in the world, negotiating with its corrupt President Mobutu.[15] Although he was no billionaire, Tempelsman—short and balding, with an elfish twinkle in his eye, an easy smile, and rosy cheeks—was wealthy and alluring.

Now that Onassis was dead, Tempelsman was keenly aware that Jackie was lonely, in need of some financial advice, and maybe even a date or two.

CHAPTER EIGHT

The
Working Woman

fter Labor Day, Tom Guinzburg finally had to reveal to his staff the secret that he had carried all summer: he had hired the most famous person in the world. Like Epstein, he knew that there would be some editors and young employees who would view Jackie as competition, a distraction, an insult, or an unapproachable icon. He knew that some of them would inevitably think, *How could this chronic shopper, this socialite, this woman who has not had a real job in more than two decades, simply waltz in here and do what I'm doing—or take the position I wanted?*

Before he told them, he turned to a young, friendly editorial assistant, Rebecca Singleton, who had arrived at Viking two years before, straight from college in Georgia, where she had majored in literature. She had impressed her colleagues from the start and Guinzburg had been nurturing her talent and ambition by allowing her to originate two nonfiction projects. He liked her ideas. He saw her potential and had noticed how grounded she was, a rare trait in the hothouse, sometimes backbiting atmosphere of New York publishing. Unlike many of her Ivy League coworkers, Becky, as many called her, was uninhibited by ideology. She was a single working girl in the big city, just like Mary Tyler Moore, but she approached her job with eagerness and practicality, not the feminist zeal that some of the other editorial assistants had, the kind that made them refuse to get coffee for anyone, or admit that they did not know something. There were already three female editors at Viking at the time, in Singleton's eyes a sign that the workplace "war" was over. Singleton stood out from the pack for other reasons: she already had had other job experiences, as a bookstore clerk, a waitress, and a nurse's aide in a psychiatric ward—all of which, oddly, would prepare her for what was about to happen.

Guinzburg knew that in order for Jackie to be successful, she needed an amanuensis to help her in the office. Singleton was resilient, had a sense of humor, and she was pretty well liked in the other departments. Perhaps she could help the staff warm to Jackie, too.

He called Singleton into his office.

There's a new editor about to start, he told her. Jackie Onassis. I want you to work for her. I know the last thing you want is another editor to report to. It won't be easy, but you have the qualities needed for such a challenge. You're going to have to handle a lot of stuff.

Guinzburg understood what that meant more than Singleton did.

While the young employee was shocked, she also knew immediately that there was no way she could turn down Guinzburg's request. It was not because she wanted to work for a famous person, but because she liked *him*. Period.

I understand, she told him.[1]

She returned to her desk as Guinzburg called the rest of the editorial department into the conference room, hoping his publishing family would accept a new in-law.

When the meeting ended, two of the other editorial assistants came by Singleton's desk.

"Well," said one, "I guess you're going to have a lot of extra work."

That night, Singleton called a friend to tell her who her new boss would be.

There was a long silence on the other end of the phone as her friend contemplated the reason for someone so rich and famous to go to work at a publishing house.

"Why?"

On the fourth Monday of September, Jackie woke up and ate a boiled egg, fortifying herself for an important day. Over the weekend, as if it were one last fling before it was time to get serious, she had attended a Frank Sinatra concert—with Frank Sinatra. It was she who received the standing ovation.

Montauk was only a few weeks ago, but its memory was fading fast, overpowered by Manhattan's energized transition to fall. Instead of heading straight to Radcliffe, Caroline chose to break free of Massachusetts for a while and enrolled in a ten-month decorative arts program, which would start soon, on October 1, at Sotheby's in London. John was back at Collegiate, the exclusive boys-only day school on the Upper West Side, close enough to keep an eye on. Jackie had been putting the finishing touches on her country house in New Jersey and had signed on to the Shriver for President committee. It was a new beginning for her, too, and she must have had a few butterflies in her stomach that morning. She pulled on a gray shirtdress, grabbed her glasses, and allowed the doorman to hail her a cab.

"Six-twenty-five Madison Avenue," she told the driver.

It was her first day on the job—her first day "working" since Jack had proposed. She was forty-six and, as the nastier gossip columnists like to point out, her face was starting to show it.

Besides Dorothy Schiff's proposal in 1964 to make her a columnist, Jackie had had other job offers. While she was still mourning JFK's death, some even joked that her "job" should be to marry Adlai Stevenson in order to turn him into a viable presidential candidate. Publicly, she shrunk from any suggestion about a second act, saying, "I'll just retire to Boston, and

September 18, 1975. Frank Sinatra escorts Jackie out
of the Uris Theater in New York via the stage door,
where he was performing, on their way to dinner.
(Bettman/CORBIS)

try to convince John Jr. that his father was president." Understandably, her children became her sole focus.

In 1973 she had considered taking a lucrative gig anchoring an NBC television show about Venice and Angkor Wat. But Onassis had vetoed the idea.

"No Greek wife works," he huffed.[2]

She was no longer a Greek wife.

Fashion houses asked her to be a spokeswoman or design her own line. Once she had told a reporter, "I was reading Carlyle and he said you should do the duty that lies nearest you. And the thing that lies nearest me is the children."[3] Now, the kids were practically gone. As Jackie's cab pulled up outside of Viking, being an editor was the duty nearest her.

Singleton, upstairs in her cubicle awaiting Jackie's arrival, was having a fashion emergency. She usually wore jeans to the office but on this occasion had chosen a denim jumper with a shirt and stockings, which had just snagged and run. She hastily shellacked her leg with clear nail polish and dashed down in the elevator, trailing noxious fumes.

Guinzburg had warned Singleton that there would be photographers, but she was utterly unprepared for the pandemonium on the other side of the elevator doors: fifty journalists—cameras, TV crews. There was Mrs. Onassis sailing in. As Jackie crossed the threshold, her transformation into a working woman was symbolic of one of the greatest shifts in American life since the Industrial Revolution, with 40 percent of women then in the workforce, a number that was increasing every day. That first step inside the building transformed her into a working woman, a new breed that was being celebrated, questioned, and picked apart in magazines, at cocktail parties, and on playgrounds across America.

Jackie did not seem to be weighed down by the history she was dragging behind her. She wore her glasses and her smile as a perfect mask. Singleton saw that this was not exactly a rescue mission she had to perform. Jackie was used to being mobbed. But Singleton—in her first of many protective acts—pushed her way through the crowd, introduced herself, grabbed Jackie by the arm, and led her to the elevator. Jackie ignored the media, never stopped to pose. She acted as if Singleton were her best friend and the only person in the lobby. And she started to babble. Jackie talked and talked and never stopped as they waited for the elevator, a monologue that did not cease on the ride up to the sixteenth floor. The chatter seemed to be a nervous reflex, or perhaps a defensive one. If she kept talking, no one would interrupt her with an inane or awkward question—the kind ordinary people ask when they become unhinged in the presence of a famous person.

Singleton did not pay much attention to the headlines during college about Jackie's buying sprees and marriage to Onassis. And she had missed out on the era of the Kennedy mystique because she was in junior high school during the Camelot years when, by her own account, she "wasn't sophisticated" and was "more of a bookworm."[4] But Singleton had been paying more attention lately, trying to understand her new boss. Over the weekend, there were reports and photographs of Jackie attending the Sinatra concert and having dinner with him at 21 after his performance.[5] With few preconceived notions, Singleton was still surprised by this beaming, energetic, and seemingly sincere woman: a woman who acted like it was her first day at school, a woman who was going on and on and about how thrilled she was with the idea of being able to create books and what an opportunity this was and she was so excited to learn the basics of editing and publishing and her children were teasing her about not knowing anything!

When the elevator opened on the sixteenth floor, the Viking office and Singleton's desk were right there. There was no additional layer of security, not even an extra door. There was no intercom system. Singleton suddenly realized that she—and she alone—had in several ways replaced the Secret Service and Onassis's Pinkerton guards as Jackie's front line of defense.

Singleton began her cursory tour by showing off her own little cubicle, piled high with manuscripts. The mound of mail caught Jackie's attention.

"It's already started," Singleton told Jackie.

"I'm sorry," Jackie groaned, rolling her eyes.

"It's OK," Singleton fibbed. "I'm looking forward to it."

Singleton explained the phone system to her—mostly that there wasn't one. She led her to a simple office nearby—smaller than most—with a window. Jackie scanned her standard-issue desk, a typewriter, filing cabinets, and a couple of chairs. She appreciated how small a publisher this was and believed it would be a good fit. Viking may have been making it up as it went along, but its lack of structure meant there would be lots of opportunities to learn.

Guinzburg, meanwhile, had been scheming to commemorate the day—for him as well as for Jackie. What better way than surprising her with a portrait sitting in front of Alfred Eisenstaedt, the father of photojournalism, who had taken the iconic photograph of the sailor kissing the nurse in Times Square when World War II had ended. Eisenstaedt was setting up in the conference room while Guinzburg went into Jackie's office to greet her, immediately struck by how happy and relaxed she seemed. He whisked her away to introduce her to the other department heads, who already were feeling resentful. After that, she sat down at a burled wood table in the book-lined conference room and posed for Eisenstaedt, who had placed some picture books—including one of his own—as a resting prop for her left hand, which was still wearing what appeared to be wedding rings. In another photo, Guinzburg, balding with longish gray sideburns at forty-nine, stood behind her, posing casually with a tie but no jacket.

When Eisenstaedt was done, Guinzburg took her to lunch at the Plaza and then granted some interviews.

McCall's wanted to know how Jackie's frequent flying to London, Gstaad, or Acapulco would square with a full-time job.

September 22, 1975. In the Viking Press offices, the newly hired editor sits with Viking's Thomas Guinzburg, the man who hired her. *(Bettman/ CORBIS)*

"She'd be sure to come back with a book," Guinzburg said. "People tend to think of her today as Mrs. Onassis. But remember Jacqueline Kennedy in Paris at the Élysée Palace with Charles de Gaulle and touring the Louvre with André Malraux. She was a cultural force for a whole generation—and she can be again."

To *Newsweek*, he offered this understatement: "One is not unmindful of the range of contacts that lady has."

Jackie was also low-key, telling a reporter: "I expect to learn the ropes at first. You sit in editorial conferences, you discuss general things, maybe you're assigned to a special project of your own. Really, I expect to be doing what my employer tells me to do."

On Jackie's second day on the job, Barbara Burn, a special projects editor at Viking, took Jackie to lunch at Guinzburg's suggestion to explain to her exactly what the role of a consulting editor was. Burn had made a reservation at the Carlyle Hotel, a location that would have made it easy for Jackie to head home after lunch, which Burn assumed she would.[6]

"Burn, [party of] two," she told the host, when they arrived. The staff immediately cleared a large table and sat the women. Jackie ordered a salad. But the staff was so unnerved trying to respect her space that she had to eat her lunch with an iced tea spoon because no one saw her looking for a fork.

Jackie got down to business. "Look," she said to Burn, "the only other consulting editor at Viking is Malcolm Cowley. I couldn't begin to do what he does."

Cowley had covered World War I for the *Pittsburgh Post-Gazette*, was part of the literary scene in Paris with Hemingway and Fitzgerald in the 1920s, and chronicled the expat scene. He had written a couple of acclaimed books and at Viking had pushed to publish Kerouac's *On the Road*.

"So I don't know exactly what I'm supposed to do," she told Burn.

"Start by reading manuscripts and writing evaluations," Burn told her.

When the check came, Jackie paid for it. But Burn, still in the mode of teaching Jackie the ropes of publishing, told her to "be sure to keep the receipt."

"Oh, never mind, I paid in cash."

"No, no," Burn said. "You're supposed to charge it and keep the receipt."

On the walk back to the office, Burn was struck by how the masses of people parted before them, staring. Jackie never made eye contact, but did not complain.[7]

Once the world knew where Jackie worked, the office was deluged—with manuscripts, forty to fifty unsolicited ones per day; crazy phone calls from people asking her for money; adoring mail containing locks of hair; and new interpretations of the Kennedy assassinations. One woman sent in a portrait of her grandchild—dead, in a casket—because she said she had remembered when Jackie lost a child. Singleton intercepted such things.[8] But she was becoming increasingly nervous about it and told Jackie what was happening.

"Throw it away," Jackie told her. "Rose Kennedy responds to every card, every letter she gets about Jack or Bobby. She sends back a prayer card . . . You just can't encourage that kind of thing. I know it sounds cruel but it's better not to encourage it."

Singleton appreciated that there was no sense perpetuating the myth. But not every request was so easily dispatched.

One morning, around 10:00, the receptionist called Singleton to the visitor's waiting area because there was a large man there who wanted to see Jackie. When Singleton saw him, he told her he had dynamite strapped to him. Singleton could thank her psychiatric nursing experiences for being unflappable at that moment. She patted him down, was relieved to find nothing alarming, and accepted the manuscript he had brought for Jackie before loading him onto an elevator. Just as she did that, another elevator opened, disgorging a man dressed as clergy, who had also shown up a few times before saying it was his wish before he died to see Jackie. Singleton had a persuasive conversation with him and ushered that man back around to the elevator as well.

When Singleton returned to her cubicle, the phones were ringing. Tabloids had been increasing their cash offers for interviews, to no effect. But then Singleton was surprised to answer the phone and have Mike Wallace's secretary on the line.

"I have Mr. Wallace on the phone for you," she said.

Singleton, feminist or no, was annoyed that he had made his secretary call, and worse, the woman referred to her boss as "Mr. Wallace," whose voice was suddenly booming through the receiver.

"Hi, Becky," he said.

Two strikes, she thought. Becky? Not even Rebecca?

"How are we gonna get Jackie on *60 Minutes*?" Wallace asked.

Singleton was completely unmoved—he had blown it at

"hello"—and she was enjoying the fact that he was surprised by her solid refusal.

Wallace wasn't the only one who was off the mark calling her Becky. Once, she wistfully remarked to Jackie that she really preferred the name Rebecca. Jackie laughed, then told her that she had never really been fond of "Jackie," and preferred Zhack-LEEN, the French pronunciation, but oh well. Regardless, they continued to refer to each other by Jackie and Becky and laughed about it.

After Singleton hung up with Wallace, a regular gadfly was on the phone asking to speak with Jackie.

"I'm sorry, she is not available," Singleton said.

"Then I would like a detailed description of what she's wearing."

Singleton declined.

The next caller said she wanted Jackie to know that a noted theater critic had parked his van in front of 1040 Fifth and was stealing her furniture. Singleton hung up.

But one threat was serious enough to warrant the FBI to spend the day there just in case the person rang again. He didn't.

Not all of those seeking to meet Jackie were unstable. The author J. P. Donleavy made an appointment to see her, saying he was writing a book about fox hunting and could he speak to her about it? Jackie thought the request was odd, so she had Burn sit in on the meeting. But Burn had never fox hunted and so once she knew it was safe, Burn left them to talk. After Donleavy left, Jackie told Burn, "It was fine. I think he just wanted to meet me."[9]

Jackie wasted no time settling into a routine and attempting to stifle any perception that she was a dilettante.[10] She arrived by taxi between 9:30 and 10:00 AM, greeted the receptionist on the sixteenth floor—"Good morning, Patty," "Good morning, Mrs. Onassis"—and then said hello to Singleton.

"Good morning, Becky!"

"Good morning, Jackie."

She poured her own coffee into a paper cup with a plastic holder. There was an office rule: the first person in had to brew the coffee. One morning, Richard Barber, director of publicity at Viking, arrived to find Jackie wrestling on the floor with a bag of coffee trying to open it. She sheepishly handed it him. He opened it. And then she took it back to brew a pot for the office.[11]

Back at her desk, the in-box would be stuffed with manuscripts that Singleton had screened to weed out the bad and the crafty—those seeking some sort of autographed response.

Singleton complained to Jackie about these blatant attempts to get a response just to say they got one from Jackie.

"OK," Jackie said, about to show her sense of humor. "These ones that are really important or supposedly important, you sign those and I'll sign some of yours."

They forged each other's signatures until they each got very good at it. Singleton shredded the little notes that Jackie sent her, such as "Write him 'no'" or "Tell him 'yes.'" She didn't want anyone fishing through the wastebasket for a memento.

Singleton also screened her calls. Whenever a rumor rippled through the media, the switchboard would light up.

"Is it true that Jackie is playing a witch in an Italian movie?"

"No."

"Did she really sign Frank Sinatra's autobiography for $1 million?"

"Categorically not true but we're all trying."

"Is she going to marry Frank Sinatra?"

"Categorically untrue and not trying." [12]

In addition to checking her in-box, Jackie would read a circulating file filled with pink carbon paper showing how colleagues had responded to literary agents and other editors. She would do this while chewing gum at her desk—an oral diversion from smoking or biting her nails. But when she'd get up to go to an editorial meeting, she'd realize she still had gum in her mouth and pop it into a tissue like a high school girl before class.

"I can't go in to see the boss chewing gum!" she'd squeal to Singleton, who, walking beside her noted that Jackie enjoyed such gestures of deference, an instinctive way of being respectful without diminishing herself.

She was also humble in a way that generated respect, making her own photocopies, doing most of her own typing, and keeping her office door open. She dressed in plain slacks, sweater ensembles, and simple or no jewelry, though she had museum-worthy baubles. With the exception of the Earth Shoes she sometimes wore, Singleton noted that Jackie dressed like everyone else—"just a little bit better."

Jackie would leave around 4:30. She worked at home, at night, and sometimes on weekends.

Within a week, she had written a six-page memo with about thirty book ideas on a wide range of subject matters, typed with space between them to allow room for her colleagues to comment as she passed it among them and asked for their feedback.

In a sense, she was exposing her belly, showing them she was smart, but respecting them and their experience. It was a politically astute move, providing a release valve for the fear some of the other editors had that Jackie's books would be published over theirs. Their feedback to Jackie was honest. *Well, this book already exists,* said one. *That is similar to another book out there,* wrote another. Many of the ideas were "lovely"—Singleton's word—but unprofitable, including producing the work of a modern Greek poet whom Jackie had met through Onassis.

Jackie also sent a memo to the junior books department suggesting something on "word derivatives from Greek and Latin," a coloring book "tracing the history of gold in the world," and "an archeology coloring book" with hinged pages.[13] The response, written in memo form to "JKO," thanked her for the ideas but said they were "not the type of thing" Viking would publish and "not the kind of book" that department was interested in.

While she was generally delighted with the job, she was beginning to show signs of impatience. Publishing moved slowly. She wanted a project. Even with Jackie being Jackie, it took a long time to woo a big name like Frank Sinatra. Attending a concert and dinner was just a kind of foreplay.

Guinzburg had thought for a long time about how to help Jackie learn without her having a public failure. One option was to plug her into books that were already in motion. But before the month was over, Muffie Brandon (now Cabot), the wife of Henry Brandon, the *Sunday Times* of London's Washington bureau chief, came to Viking to meet with Guinzburg and pitch an idea based on an American bicentennial traveling exhibit of artifacts meant to celebrate women's roles in the nation's history. When Brandon arrived at the publishing house, she was pleased to walk in the room and see Jackie there, waiting with Guinzburg.

The two had known each other for years. And Brandon had bet that the idea would appeal to the new editor's strengths: her interest in and knowledge of history, and the ability to pull together themes and content with art. Although the topic sounded dusty, in truth it was politically edgy and even intellectual. She explained that she had been working with a curator to pull together the exhibit, called *Remember the Ladies: Women in America, 1750 to 1815,* after a line from a letter that Abigail Adams wrote to her husband, John, when he was president. It made sense to do such a book now, not only to celebrate the nation's two hundredth birthday but also because there was a growing interest in women's stories that were at risk of being forgotten. *Ms.* magazine even had a regular column at the time called Lost Women.

Jackie's eyes sparkled as Brandon told her about the project and she sat forward in her chair. For two hours, she asked "penetrating" questions.

Finally, Guinzburg turned to Jackie.

"What do you think?"

"Oh, let's do it!" she said.

Before Brandon left, Jackie gave her a tour of the office—and they agreed to meet again to start sifting through materials.

The *Remember the Ladies* team consisted of curator Conover Hunt, writer and academic Linda Grant De Pauw, and researcher Miriam Schneir. They were on a tight deadline, hoping to debut the exhibit and the book the following spring in Plymouth, Massachusetts, at the home site of Mercy Otis Warren, a Revolutionary-era writer. And so with time short, the group had scheduled a meeting at Viking with Burn, who did much of the work and who had negotiated the contract, to begin laying out the many pictures and captions for the book. It was a book with a clear agenda, explained in the introduction:

The years between 1750 and 1815 witnessed the passing of a remarkable generation of women who were strong, self-reliant, employed in all occupations entered by men, although not in equal numbers, and active in political and military affairs. Ironically, the conditions that enabled the United States to establish itself as an independent nation that had permitted middle-class white men to achieve greater wealth and political power forced women into a more restricted role.

Singleton led Brandon, Hunt, and Schneir to a windowless room where they met Burn—their day-to-day contact—and Lewis P. Lewis, who was managing editor of Studio Books, the picture book division of Viking. They splayed photos on the carpeted floor and were crawling among the images when Jackie walked in wearing black slacks, a white silk blouse, black shoes, and long gold chains.

Jackie joined them on the floor and looked closely at the images: a drawing of a colonial woman in a tricorn hat with a rifle by her hip, a 1777 engraving of an old maid with a cat, and a portrait of a mother grieving over a dead child. Jackie's ambition, fear, and life experience all seemed to be reflected in these antique illustrations.

Jackie heard that everyone had already agreed with the content structure of the chapters; that decision had been settled early because a photographer had to take color pictures of the items. The chapters would allow readers to explore the progress or lack thereof that women had made since the American Revolution. One chapter in particular, "Women at Work," seemed particularly relevant at that moment on the floor at Viking, with the Equal Rights Amendment again up for Congressional ratification.

But two other issues needed to be resolved: how to handle the captions and what would be the size and look of the book?

"I think you ought to do it flush left/ragged right," Hunt said of the caption layout.

"Let's talk about that," said Jackie, unfamiliar with the publishing term that meant the text would align on the left and be uneven on the right.

Perhaps with the exception of Brandon, who had been in regular contact with Jackie about the book, the sight and sound of "Mrs. Onassis" shocked Hunt even though she expected her to be there. Hunt was surprised that her voice was not breathy. She was thinner and more fragile looking than her iconic image allowed. Her humor was sharp and she warmed up immediately when anyone mentioned her kids. But perhaps what stood out more than anything was that Jackie was an apprentice, listening closely to the discussion and asking a lot of questions, even about basic things, like typography.

Hunt was also moved by the sight of seeing Jackie work, a powerful image for the women's movement and a sign of change. And she was moved to be part of Jackie's first book. This was a woman, Hunt thought, who was no expert—not yet anyway—but she had some of the greatest contacts in the world, and had used her influence to get this book to Viking, which meant that most of the authors' expenses were paid, more copies would be published, and there was advertising behind the project. Hunt couldn't help but think that 1975 was a period when a lot of women were undergoing big transformations in their lives and Jackie was no exception. Sure, she was alone, had a ton of money and nearly grown children, all things that would allow her to design a life that would bring her happiness. But this is what she chose: a seat on the floor of a tiny publisher, discussing history, photography, and design.

Hunt pulled herself out of her private monologue to focus again on the captions.

"I would like a classic curatorial caption, which says, 'This is the object and this is what it is made of, these are the measurements, this is where it was made, when it was made, who owns it.' And below that you put your content so they tell their own story. I don't want to have to use a lot of reference numbers, like 'See Figure I.'"

"Fine," Jackie said.

As the meeting wrapped up, Jackie said she was excited about the project.

"This is going to be something!" she said.

Brandon said she was working on the logistics for the Plymouth opening and was hoping then First Lady Betty Ford would do the honors.

"I'd love to be a fly on the wall," Jackie said, triggering laughter in the room.

"Of course we'd love to have you," Brandon said. But Jackie demurred, saying she did not want to disrupt things in such a small town.

Then she left, just before the two-hour meeting ended.[14]

Jackie would have other meetings with Brandon, including one where they both laughed hard trying to figure out how to illustrate an eighteenth-century sex manual that was supposed to be part of the book. Jackie also insisted on including information about a root women chewed to induce abortion. She did not have much to say when they came to the section on first ladies from the period, except she did respond to a couple of lines from Martha Washington. One read: "I lead a dull life—a state prisoner." Jackie laughed at that one. The other: Georgetown "is a dirty hole."

"It still is," Jackie said.[15]

Jackie slowly made friends at work, ingratiating herself by asking questions. It is no surprise that she gravitated toward Bryan Holme, head of Studio Books. Holme, an Englishman who was older than Jackie, was considered a visual genius. Jackie found his work appealing and he quickly realized how good her eye was. Often, he would stick his head in Singleton's cubicle, ask for Jackie, and say, *There's something I want to show her!*

They would eventually find projects to work on together—including a photo book on the Civil War photographer and Abraham Lincoln portrait taker Mathew Brady, and an illustrated book called *In the Russian Style,* published the following year with Jackie's name—the only one—on the cover as editor, about imperial clothing and other possessions.

Jackie also established a strong relationship with Corlies Smith, known as "Cork." He was tall, wrapped in tweed, and smoke unfiltered Pall Malls. He was also witty, dry, and deeply respected for spotting talent, including his author Thomas Pynchon. Jackie and Smith ate together frequently; she soaked up his wisdom, and Smith, who liked to down several martinis over lunch, was secure enough in his accomplishments to know that she posed no threat.

Still she was having a tougher time winning over colleagues whose default position from her first day was skeptical, bordering on hostile. She tried hard to find gestures that would appeal to them, such as offering tickets to the next summer's Democratic National Convention, where she would be onstage. But for those who did not respond to her overtures, she did not try again.

CHAPTER NINE

The Empty Nester

Jackie was settling into her new routine at work and just getting to know the weekend house in northern New Jersey that she had bought almost twelve months earlier—a place that would have been completed sooner if it weren't for the past year's tribulations. She had hoped the house would be a new kind of island sanctuary—a place hidden by trees of the Great Eastern Forest with a private web of trails for her to ride on. The decorators had done a nice job filling the converted barn with big sofas in happy prints of orange, lemon, lime, peach, apricot and plum.[1] The place was comfortable and welcoming, beckoning her over the George Washington Bridge as she drove her "jellybean green" BMW.

On top of the new house and the new job, she was also now

dealing with the new reality that Caroline had just moved to London.[2]

The tight threesome of Jackie, John, and Caroline was loosening and it was difficult for Jackie, as it is for many parents, to let go. But it was even more difficult for her. As a single mother with children whose last name was Kennedy, she had always tried to overcompensate for the parent who was gone while pushing her kids to achieve great things. When they were young, Jackie instructed their nannies to speak to them in their native foreign languages. She wanted her children to play musical instruments, to try sports—be it tennis or ballet. She also made sure they had a "normal" life, ensuring they were invited to parties thrown by friends who may have been too intimidated to ask for their company.

Caroline had been at Concord Academy, a boarding school that was only a few hours away by car. Now, she was on the other side of the Atlantic Ocean, in a world that Jackie still knew was dangerous. Caroline was a lot like Jackie—sharp-witted, soft-spoken, and stubborn—with similar interests in art and literature. For Caroline's eighth birthday, Jackie asked her what she wanted. The girl requested the writer George Plimpton—thirty-eight years old at the time—to come to her party at Hammersmith Farm. She got him.

Caroline had spent much of her youth in controlled environments: gated in the White House, tracked by Secret Service agents, cloistered behind layers of security at 1040 Fifth, and attending school in Massachusetts as a *Kennedy*, which in a sense made her everyone's child. She was supposed to have started at Radcliffe for her freshman year of college but had changed her mind—finally ready to experience life far away from her mother's understandably watchful eye. She wanted freedom, even if just for a year, from following the family's well-worn path. She wanted freedom from the Kennedy name, and from the Kennedy geography, which was especially centered in Boston and Cambridge, cities that were, at that very moment, squabbling over which one should become the home of the JFK presidential library. She wanted freedom from the expectation that if she went abroad to study, it would be at the Sorbonne.

And so Jackie was left in New York with John, who was still attending the exclusive and highly competitive boys-only Collegiate School, a mere crosstown bus ride away, behind its club-like red doors. There, students referred to one another by their often-famous last names and assumed many of their classmates would go to Harvard—just like them. Unlike Caroline, John was a mystery to his mother, especially at this stage of life. A rebellious teenager with bushy hair and a goofy nature who could be disruptive in class, Jackie found it difficult to relate to him one-on-one. She was exasperated trying to have a conversation with him. Singleton, who had a sister close in age to John, told Jackie about a minor craze for a young-adult book by Peter Beagle that Viking had published called *The Last Unicorn*.

"Ask him about it," she suggested, after Jackie had confessed to being at her wit's end with the boy.

That night, Jackie brought up the topic at the dinner table

and John knew all about it. She thanked Singleton for helping her connect with her son.

With or without conversation, Jackie and John spent many quiet nights at home. She helped him with his homework and she did her own, poring over manuscripts, drafting memos. She rarely attended social events, despite the many tempting invitations she had. And when she did, they were intellectual forums, fund-raising committee meetings, or publishing gatherings. In her spare time, she jogged in Central Park, practiced yoga, and went for weekly psychotherapy sessions.

In London, Jackie had made arrangements for Caroline to stay at the Kensington home of Sir Hugh Fraser while the girl looked for a more permanent apartment. Fraser, a Tory member of Parliament who had known JFK since Joe Kennedy's days as ambassador to London, was married to Antonia Fraser, an author friend of Jackie's. The Frasers had five teenage children of their own, and were happy to host Caroline, with Fraser personally driving her to class on his way to work each day. But on October 23, Fraser's usual 8:30 AM departure time was delayed by a phone call with another MP. Caroline, waiting in the drawing room, was looking idly out the window at Fraser's red Jaguar and saw a neighbor walking his two poodles, pausing to look at a package in the gutter, when an explosion threw Caroline on her back. Fraser, who was still in his pajamas, was propelled from his chair by the percussion that crashed the windows. Outside was a horrible scene. Fraser's car was shredded, in flames, and upended on its roof. The neighbor's torso had landed in the garden while his legs had been blasted to the other side of the road. The wrought iron fence was blown in, and the blast felt a half mile away. Adding to the chaos was the sound of sirens blaring that awful high-pitched wale of European ambulances and police cars.

Scotland Yard believed the bomb had been planted by the Irish Republican Army and was meant for Fraser, who frequently spoke out against terrorism. No one thought the target was the now-dead neighbor—a renowned cancer specialist—and certainly not for Caroline, who, deeply shaken, was whisked to a nearby house for safekeeping by police.

"There is no doubt it was meant for me," Fraser said. "Somebody obviously wants to blow me up. I am not surprised. I can think of a lot of people who would want to blow me up." [3]

Jackie, roused from sleep at 1040 Fifth by yet another heart-thumping transatlantic phone call at an hour that would cause an adrenaline rush for anyone, could hardly believe the words she was hearing. More violence. More death. Was anyone safe anywhere? Since the assassination, Jackie was so shell-shocked that she couldn't even watch anything remotely disturbing on television. Now here she was listening to her daughter explain that if Sir Fraser had just gotten dressed and out the door on time, she would have been blown to bits.

Jackie wanted her home immediately. Caroline didn't want to leave just as the school year was beginning, though. And besides, she was not the target. Jackie pleaded with Scotland Yard to provide protection for the girl, who was a month shy of her eighteenth birthday, but they refused.[4] Jackie was being forced to let go. If Caroline was going to stay, she at least had to agree to one demand: she could not live in her own apartment. Instead, she moved in with her uncle Stash Radziwill, and tried to put the incident behind her.

Caroline was saddened by the neighbor's death and the continually unnerving acts by the IRA, but she seemed to personify the British mantra: keep calm and carry on. There seemed to be lots of fun things and interesting people in swinging London, where she spent her days wearing blue corduroys, a turtleneck, and scuffed suede shoes to study at the National Gallery or at Sotheby's on New Bond Street. At night London gave New York some stiff competition. Queen was singing "Bohemian Rhapsody" at the Hammersmith Odeon, with Freddie Mercury in a white satin jumpsuit. Led Zeppelin was at Earl's Court. There were supper clubs like Tramp, packed with Bright Young Things, and at Annabels, people were doing a new dance called the Hustle. There were plays and movies, and dinners at Claridge's. Caroline had invitations from the rich, famous, and noble, with the Fraser kids adding to the introductions around the city. There were trips to country estates. There were boys. And there were big plans percolating for her eighteenth birthday in November. As always, there were paparazzi trailing her most mundane acts, like having a sandwich with friends after class. On one of these occasions, annoyed by the photographers

Caroline walking on a rain-soaked street on her way to a course at Sotheby's after house hunting with her mother, London, England.

(Express/Getty Images)

on the other side of the café window, she carried a glass of water outside and threw it in the face of one of the cameramen, elevating the situation to a news story that her mother scolded her about.[5] In fact, Jackie was increasingly alarmed by Caroline's behavior and partying. Scale back the birthday party, she told her. Buckle down. You may be in London, but you're still a Kennedy.

Meanwhile, in New York, the Committee to Save Grand Central was still in a public relations battle. Having opened a storefront near the terminal in August, the group was selling $6 polyester neckties with red or golden bitten apples on them, representing the slogan, "No More Bites Out of the Big Apple." They were hoping to build more support for the city when it made its case on October 21, arguing that the terminal's landmark status should be upheld.[6] In the weeks that it would take the court to decide the case, Jackie kept busy outside of work. She toured the city room of the *New York Post* with her old friend Dorothy Schiff, who was now encouraging her to run for the Senate. She attended an affair to honor the writer Lillian Hellman. She was on the town with novelist Philip Roth. She hosted a first-anniversary fund-raiser for the International Center for Photography, arriving with Karl Katz, her "intellectual boyfriend." In keeping with the more subdued look she had recently adopted, Jackie wore a black Ungaro tunic and pants to the event, stocked with people such as Doris Duke and Marella Agnelli. The focus of the night was an exhibit by Ernst Haas, a pioneer in color photography. After dinner, she raised her glass to thank a few people, went downstairs to listen to a bit of Japanese music, and left in low-key fashion.[7]

Even her lunch venues were quieter, which was not surprising after what Truman Capote had just written in the November issue of *Esquire*, a roman à clef called "La Côte Basque 1965" about high society, how vacuous it was, how obsessed it was with where they sat, with whom, and who else was there. Capote's piece centered on having lunch with the fictitious Lady Ina Coolbirth at the famous restaurant while famous people trickled in. The subtitle of the piece was "Where the *plat du jour* is seated somewhere in sight." Of course, his words stabbed and sliced like cutlery. In one scene, Jackie and Lee—their real names published—arrive and take their seats.

> *Lady Ina observed: "You can see those girls have swung a few big deals in their time. I know many people can't abide either of them, usually women, and I can understand that because they don't like women and almost never have anything good to say about any woman. But they're perfect with men, a pair of perfect geisha girls; they know how to keep a man's secrets and how to make him feel important. If I were a man, I'd fall for Lee myself."* [8]

Capote's voice in the article then goes on to recall a night at a drag queen contest in Harlem.

Chorus boys and bank cashiers and Irish elevator boys got up as Marilyn Monroe, as Audrey Hepburn, as Jackie Kennedy. Indeed Mrs. Kennedy was the most popular inspiration; a dozen boys, the winner among them, wore her high-rise hair-do, winged eyebrows, sulky, palely-painted mouth. And in life that is how she struck me—not as a bona fide woman, but as an artful female impersonator impersonating Mrs. Kennedy.[9]

The story ends with Lady Coolbirth disclosing that she is getting a divorce. "But I can't live without a man," she says half-drunk on Cristal. "Women like me have no other focus, no other way of scheduling our lives. Even if we hate him, even if he's an iron head with a cotton heart, it's better than this footloose routine."[10]

What Capote was suggesting in his piece was that some women—even in 1975—would never be happy alone, without a rich husband. It was as if he was needling not only Jackie but Lee, who had left Sarah Lawrence College in her sophomore year to marry Michael Canfield, moved to London, got divorced, married a prince, had two kids, decorated a couple of fabulous homes, and tried acting, playing Laura in *The Philadelphia Story* onstage in Chicago. *Time*'s review of her performance said she was "only slightly less animated than the portrait of herself that hung over the mantel." By 1972 Lee decided it was time to move back to New York, without her husband, and they split themselves and the kids: Anthony stayed in England and Tina came back with Lee, settling in an apartment overlooking Central Park three blocks from Jackie.

Lee and Jackie did not look much alike, but they were close in other ways—talking on the phone most every day, having lunch regularly, and sharing vacations. Now they were geographically connected, with their lives taking on an odd parallel. Their kids were similar ages. Their second marriages were over, with Lee's divorce final in July 1974. Both sisters, so accustomed to being defined by men, had to find their own way to make it. Lee landed a gig with CBS doing interviews with famous people, most of whom happened to be her friends. In one episode, she asked Rudolph Nureyev, an openly gay ballet dancer, if he ever planned to get married. "One doesn't expect close friends to ask such silly questions," he said, blushing. Of Halston, another guest on her show, she asked what clothes women could buy for $25. "Nothing," he said. The network canceled the program after six episodes.

Lee also considered going into newspaper journalism, the profession her sister had loved, but instead she set about writing memoirs of her childhood. The manuscript was due to Delacorte Press in October 1975. That project had prompted an attic expedition that unearthed the old scrapbook, *One Special Summer*, which Delacorte had recently published. The new memoir, which she was plotting out in longhand in a spiral notebook, seemed a lot harder to write than the travelogue. Delacorte had given her a reported $250,000 advance, and Lee was granting interviews so that people knew she was working on it.

"People always write about me as the girl who has everything," Lee huffed to *McCall's*. "They always ask this silly

question, 'Why should the girl who has everything do anything?' It's so unfair. Gloria Steinem says they do that only
'cause you're a woman. They'd never do that to a man, and to a
large extent, I think that's true."

Still, what would Lee do? What *could* Lee do?

"I've painted but I am not a painter. Nor an actress. Nor a
writer," she told *McCall's*. "I was reading Thomas Wolfe, and
he said he was not a writer. I understand that. I know people
who have written books, but they aren't writers either. It would
be presumptuous to say I could direct, but I certainly could
do producing. I have the ability to put something together. If
something interested me enough and I thought I could do it, I'd
make a stab at it. I've never been sorry about anything I've done
in my field and I'll do it all again. I'll never find myself just staring out the window." [11]

Unlike Lee, Jackie had always been more purposeful, more
sure of herself, more able to recover.

Reading Capote's fiction, Jackie might have remembered
an interview she granted in 1972 with a newspaper in Tehran,
where Onassis was trying to work out an oil deal. A reporter
had asked her what differences there were in her two husbands.
"People often forget," she said, avoiding a more direct answer,
"that I was Jacqueline Lee Bouvier before being Mrs. Kennedy
or Mrs. Onassis." [12]

Capote was not the only one writing nasty things about
Jackie in the fall of 1975. Sally Quinn, Ben Bradlee's third wife
and a feature writer at the *Washington Post*, had practically made

a beat out of her, following her around to events that fall and summing up the post-Onassis era by responding to Capote's piece of fiction.

"This is the kind of thing that people used to say about Jackie Onassis," Quinn wrote. "It is the kind of thing that would be hard to say about her now. She is acting like a person who is interested for the first time in making herself feel important. Not important as Mrs. Kennedy or Mrs. Onassis, but as someone in her own right." But then Quinn used the journalistic disguise of her own thoughts by inserting what "skeptics" thought. And skeptics, she wrote, believed Jackie "is only following a trend, that she is going literary-journalistic because since Watergate that's where the glamour is, and the action. They say that the jet set frivolity is out and serious thinking, books and newspapers are in. In a few years they say, she will be following whatever *nouvelle vague* there is. They say she is only doing something now because it is currently fashionable for women to do something." [13]

As hard as Jackie tried to lead a life that was quieter and more intellectual, one that had a vibe of self-sufficiency and self-assuredness as a single working mother, her past kept interrupting.

When Lee began working on her memoir—ultimately never completed—exploring what her childhood on Long Island had been like, she spent some time with her aunt and cousin, both named Edith Beale, living in East Hampton at their waterfront home called Grey Gardens. But "Big Edie" and "Little Edie," like the house itself, were falling apart, in spectacular fashion.

Big Edie was a Bouvier, the sister of Jackie and Lee's father. She had married Phelan Beale and they had two sons and a daughter before he divorced her, leaving her with the house and no money. Like Jackie, little Edie had grown up privileged, and had been a Farmington debutante who lived in New York City for a while in her twenties. But her mother had insisted she return to Grey Gardens to keep her company in the big house. From that point on, the Edies spiraled away from their privileged life, passing eccentricity, and slamming into a wall of mental instability. By 1975, Little Edie was fifty-six years old (her mother seventy-nine). She wore her skirts upside down, pinning the hem so it stayed at her waist, and she wrapped sweaters on her head like a hijab, covering up the fact that she had alopecia, which caused her hair to fall out. Meanwhile, Big Edie didn't get out of her twin bed much. Propped up by pillows, occasionally only partially dressed, she ate ice cream from a tub with a plastic knife, sang like a proud Broadway star, and barked orders at her daughter. Each of these women appeared as abandoned as the shingled house, which time—and raccoons, encouraged by Little Edie's offerings of Wonder bread and Cat Chow—had extensively infiltrated. The cats, of which there were many, pissed shamelessly behind an oil portrait of Big Edie in her stunning youth, now seemingly forgotten in a corner on the floor.

Lee and Peter Beard had thought the Beales' story would

make a good film. But they couldn't finance the project. Instead they turned it over to the Maysles brothers, David and Albert, who understood immediately how sensational the setting and the characters could be on film. That they were Jackie's relatives made it all the more bizarre and delicious. In order to tolerate the flea infestation in the house, the documentarians wore flea collars around their ankles as they followed the women using a handheld camera, a style of filmmaking called direct cinema, a precursor to reality TV. The Maysleses produced a film that for ninety-four painful minutes seemed to express the anxiety of a generation of women who were bred to believe their lives would be meaningless without a husband to support them in every possible way. There, in Technicolor, the story line played out: this is what became of old maids. They filled the emptiness with trash and they filled the silence with rants and old records. The cats, of course, were like an icon in a Renaissance painting, always there in the background, symbolizing the subject's state of spinster hell.

"Mother sees me as a baby. I see myself as a little girl. The Maysleses see me as a woman," little Edie deluded to the camera.[14] The film debuted at the New York Film Festival before spreading to general theaters in the fall of 1975. There was no footage of Jackie in the movie, but it was nearly impossible for anyone to watch and not wonder how two branches of the same of the family could live such different lives. Jackie and Lee had not ignored the Beales. In 1972 they and some other relatives had spent $4,000 cleaning the house and another

$30,000 repairing the mansion as local health officials threatened to condemn it.[15] But this was one of those instances where money could not solve the problems, could not repair every hole in the Beales' lives.

If Jackie saw the movie debut, she didn't let on. But she had plenty of things happening to distract her from going to the cinema. Caroline had just arrived home for the holidays and there seemed to be a lot to be grateful for at that year's Thanksgiving feast. Jackie was thrilled to have her children there with her at the dinner table, safe and sound. Her daughter would be turning eighteen the next week, on November 29, and it seemed fitting that Caroline was also preparing for her first photography exhibit, at the Lexington Labs Gallery in New York. On the night of the opening, Jackie thought about her daughter's talent and the bittersweet memories she had captured, each fleeting. On one wall was a picture of John, jumping off the *Christina*. On another was a self-portrait: Caroline dressed like a gypsy with a cigarette and a ring through her nose.[16]

Caroline's photography offered a glimpse into the past, a private world that few had seen. Jackie, meanwhile, was eager to share a glimpse of the future, inviting Caroline to come for a tour of her office at Viking. Caroline breezed in and breezed out, trailing her teasing comments behind.

"Oh you just missed Caroline," Jackie said when Singleton turned up at her desk. "She said I had an assistant who knows more than I do." Singleton knew self-deprecation was one of Jackie's ways of leveling the playing field. But she also knew that Caroline was irreverent because Jackie talked a lot about her kids, and frequently related how they joked about their mother's job.

Singleton could see how hard Jackie was trying to fit in. And she began to think about what kind of meaningful Christmas present she could give to Jackie—a woman who seemingly had everything—to thank her for being such a great boss.

On December 16, Jackie received an unexpected gift—not from Singleton but from the Appellate Division of the State Supreme Court, which ruled 3 to 2 to overturn Judge Saypol's decision. By reinstating the landmark status of Grand Central, the court denied Penn Central's plan to build an office tower on the site, saying the station was "a major part of the cultural and architectural heritage of New York City." It was a victory, but Penn Central immediately said it was considering an appeal yet again.

Jackie would have only one day of enjoying the headlines. Over the years, she had learned how to cope with her husband's assassination. She had moved away from Washington, where the mere sight of the White House would send her reeling. But this year she was caught off guard as disturbing claims began to seep into the national conversation. First was a book called *Post Mortem: JFK Assassination Cover-Up Smashed!* by Harold Weisberg that attempted to prove that the Warren Commission was wrong in its conclusion that Lee Harvey Oswald had acted alone.[17] In fact, Weisberg claimed that Oswald was not even the killer; there had been a conspiracy and a cover-up.

Into this thick atmosphere dropped another explosive revelation—one that the newly cynical media, hardened by the recent sins of Watergate and Vietnam—were happy to cover. The Senate Select Committee on Intelligence had released a report in mid-November claiming that the CIA had plotted to have the mafia kill Fidel Castro between 1960 and 1962. The report obliquely mentioned a "close friend" of the president— someone who also knew Sam Giancana, the capo of the Chicago mob, and his associate John Rosselli. The report did not provide the name or sex of this close personal friend. But the media, suspecting a partisan suppression of important facts, did. Her name was Judith Campbell Exner, a dark-haired California girl. Frank Sinatra had met her at a party and then introduced her to Kennedy in Las Vegas during the 1960 campaign, a meeting that launched a sexual relationship that lasted for two years and was chronicled with a phone log that showed seventy calls from then Judith Campbell to the White House between March of 1961 and March of 1962.

After the report was made public, Exner was so upset by what she called "wild-eyed speculation" that she had passed information from the mob to JFK that she called a press conference on December 17, 1975—the day after the court reinstated Grand Central as a landmark—at the Westgate Hotel in San Diego. Her face tan and her eyes hidden behind glasses big enough to prompt comments about her being a Jackie look-alike, Exner sat with her attorney in front of a bank of cameras and a crowd of reporters, who scribbled every word of her prepared statement. She disclosed that her relationship with JFK was entirely "of a personal nature." And she said she was upset that her involvement with the president would be mischaracterized. The relationship was about intimacy—not business.

"To me," Exner said, "he was Jack Kennedy and not the president." [18]

Back in New York, Jackie could not escape the blanket coverage of Exner's confession. The words echoed in her head and destroyed a little bit more of a dream she'd held on to. The man whose life she had been devoted to, the father of her children, the man whose legacy she was further immortalizing that very month with final plans for building the JFK Library in Boston, had carried on with some bimbo for most of his time in the White House. Jackie must have known but, like many women of her generation, had let it go. Now, how could she be any more humiliated?

Perhaps she would not have been so mortified if the Camelot myth had not existed. But the myth was a powerful one. Jackie would know. She had created it on a rain-soaked night in Hyannis Port a week after the assassination. She had asked Theodore White, a reporter for *Life* magazine, to come right away; there was something she wanted the magazine to say to the country. He arrived by limousine—no plane would fly to Cape Cod in the weather—and was greeted by Jack's sister Pat Lawford, some aides, and friends, all of whom Jackie asked to leave. She then turned to White and told him she was angry that some journalists were already assessing the president—dead less than a week! Jack's legacy should not be left to the historians, she said.

"Well then," White said. "Tell me about it."

She talked for hours, as if trying to purge herself of the grief. Some of what she related was too personal for White even to use. And then she said this: "When Jack quoted something, it was usually classical, but I'm so ashamed of myself—all I keep thinking of is this line from a musical comedy." She was referring to a Broadway production about the King Arthur legend that had debuted in 1960. "At night," she told White, "before we'd go to sleep, Jack liked to play some records; and the song he loved most came at the end of this record. The lines he loved to hear were: 'Don't let it be forgot, that once there was a spot, for one brief shining moment that was known as Camelot.'"

Camelot. Camelot. Camelot. Emotionally spent from the interview, and knowing that his editors were ringing up a huge expense by holding the presses for him, White typed quickly in a servant's room, relying heavily on Jackie's musical imagery. He let Jackie read the story as he called New York at 2:00 AM to dictate the piece from a wall-mount phone. A secret service agent in the other room burst in and complained. *"For Christ's sake, we need some sleep here!"*

One of his editors thought there was too much talk of Camelot. Jackie overheard the discussion and entered the room, handed him her penciled changes to the story, and shook her head, pleading with her eyes to keep Camelot in there. White fought on her behalf—and won.

Now Camelot—the fairy tale that Jackie had practically written—had a new ending. And she was devastated all over again. Her first vote had been for JFK. And after he died, she did not vote in the next presidential election, as if she could have only cast her ballot for one person. Regardless of what she may have known about JFK's indiscretions in real time, journalists never reported on his philandering, because, they rationalized, his adultery had nothing to do with his job. But if Exner carried information between the mob and the president, her sexual relationship with him *was* relevant *and* reportable, especially in the post-Watergate era, and especially if she called a press conference. There was no hiding anymore.

Right after the Exner news broke, Jackie went to see a friend unannounced. The friend was Karen Lerner, recently divorced from Alan Jay Lerner—the author of the musical *Camelot*. Alan Lerner had been a classmate of JFK's at Choate and Harvard. And by collapsing on Karen's couch and staring into space, perhaps Jackie thought that she could prove to herself that Camelot did exist somewhere—even if it had only been a stage production. Jackie never mentioned Exner during the visit. But Lerner understood everything that went unsaid. And it was plain for her to see that Jackie was depressed.[19]

Jackie's only salvation at that moment was work. She could lose herself in a book project. She could control it, shape it, enjoy it, and hide behind someone else's name on the cover. She needed to tend to her own legacy, as preservation activist—even the Grand Central battle would surely drag on for years—as an editor, and as a single, working woman. The Birkin bag filled with manuscripts was the only baggage worth carrying anymore.

When Christmastime came around, a simple gift from Rebecca Singleton stood out. She gave Jackie something she'd probably never wear—a softball team T-shirt that the staff typically wore to their company picnic. Singleton had rustled one up from storage and knew that Jackie would appreciate its symbolism.

"You are one of us," she told Jackie, handing her the package. "This is your official welcome. We don't know if you are going to [play] second base. But it's great having you around."

Jackie was truly home. And it was fitting that she remained in America for the holiday among the twinkling lights of Park Avenue rather than rocky shore of Skorpios. For vacation, she, John, and Caroline flew to the groomed slopes and hot tubs of Sun Valley, Idaho, instead of Gstaad. The trip to the resort mountain was comforting in the company of Ted Kennedy, his wife, Joan, and their three children, as well as two other branches of the clan: the Lawfords and the Smiths. The snow was knee-deep. The extended family agreed to pose in a horse-drawn sleigh and when a photographer asked them to all turn toward the camera, Jackie, in a black stretch ski jacket and jeans, gave a mirthful shout: "And neigh!"

EPILOGUE

For Jacqueline Kennedy Onassis, the transformation from wife and widow to public preservationist and editor was extraordinary not only on a personal level for her but also because it signaled new possibilities for women.

In 1959, Arthur Schlesinger met Jackie in Hyannis Port and noted that she was "flighty on politics" and full of "wide-eyed naïveté."[1] She believed that women were too emotional for politics and she sounded and behaved the way women of her time and place were supposed to. In a 1960 presidential campaign profile, Jackie said, "Running our home is a joy to me. I feel this is what I was made for. When it all goes smoothly—the food is good, Jack's clothes are pressed, the flowers look fresh—I have such satisfaction . . . I shop once a week at the supermarket to see what's new and to choose fresh vegetables." When asked in the same article for her favorite menu for entertaining at home she said, "I try to please the men. Since they are tired after working all day, hungry, and almost cranky. I start with a good homemade soup."[2] Never mind that she had an in-home cook—even then. Readers celebrated her words because it validated their own postwar suburban lives, where they made casseroles and vacuumed and volunteered while it was their husbands who "worked." By the time she became First Lady, she believed it was her duty to provide her husband an escape with "a climate of affection," with great parties in the White House, excellent and comforting food, and "the children in good moods."[3]

Although out of curiosity she read the weekly CIA summaries that Jack brought back from the Oval Office, ceasing to read them only because they depressed her,[4] she hid her intellect among traditional female roles, which were exaggerated by the fishbowl that was the White House. "Her friends who know her capacity and great intelligence are pleased that she has found a task to challenge them," the *Boston Globe* reported in 1961. "Her greatest innovation so far seems to be the lovely little flower arrangements."[5]

In truth, the sound of her voice masked her intelligence. She was athletic, small breasted, big footed (size 10), and dared to wear pants when many women were still wearing June Cleaver shirtwaist dresses. But she was idolized for the gowns she wore. She was translating documents for the president, helping him with his book, and saving Lafayette Square from the wrecking ball. And yet few people knew about those accomplishments.

Jackie could never have known that she would be among the last of the prefeminist first ladies, nor that a cultural revolution was coming, one in which women would be paid for their work outside the home. Today, in these postfeminist years, the mommy wars have centered on the choice of work—even though many women do not have the option. Jackie needed to work, not to pay the bills but to save her soul. Even in the White House, she had spent more on clothes in one year than her husband earned as president. In 1975, still awaiting what would be a $20 million settlement (to come in 1977) on her Onassis inheritance, her $10,000 Viking salary would have seemed paltry, but it was huge to her because she was earning it. Working was not about the money. It was about her self-worth.

As she changed, so did women in America. Jackie could have remained a Warhol portrait, a bouffant and a pillbox hat, but instead she did not shy from wearing bell-bottom jeans and a tight-fitting Henley sweater for a brisk walk down Fifth Avenue—perhaps still an icon, but not one stuck on a pedestal.

While some women feel trapped by age, she seemed liberated by it. *Passages* author Gail Sheehy once said that women are most happy between forty-five and fifty-five because menopause and the empty nest are physical signals that they are free to move on. Jackie turned forty-six in July 1975. Her nest was emptying. She had reached an age when finding one's purpose beyond raising children becomes central to happiness. Shopping's thrills are short and shallow. Parties with polite banter are surprisingly exhausting. Being a trophy for a spouse is a relationship doomed to fail. And chronic searching can take you around the world, but finding home within oneself is the most rewarding journey. And that's what Jackie did in 1975. She had even begun to lay plans for a retreat that she could truly call her own—not at the Kennedy compound in Hyannis Port, or on Onassis's island in the Aegean, but a tract of land she acquired on Martha's Vineyard, with the vast Atlantic defining the contours of her own private beach.

By the time the ball dropped in Times Square on New Year's Eve, bringing 1975 to a close, she could look back at everything she had accomplished over the course of one year, and had to believe that anything was possible. She had remained the caring mother she always was, but this year she was something more. She had reinvented herself. With the landmarking of Grand Central, she was part of an important cause, a cause that would require constant public relations efforts to keep the issue alive.

She also had a new job and she enjoyed reporting to work, laying the foundation for a publishing career that would span two decades. Her time at Viking would be formative, but short. She had a hand in seven books there, each of which said something about her interests: *In the Russian Style*, a picture book with illustrations that she selected based on her own visits to museums and palaces in what was then the Soviet Union; *Himself!: The Life and Times of Mayor Richard J. Daley*, by Eugene C. Kennedy; *Firebird and Other Russian Fairy Tales* (for which she wrote the introduction), by Boris Zvorykin; *The Face of Lincoln*, a picture book by James Mellon; *Inventive Paris Clothes, 1909–1930: A Photographic Essay*, by Diana Vreeland and Irving Penn; and *Sally Hemings: A Novel*, by Barbara Chase-Riboud, a story she had encouraged the author to write about Thomas Jefferson's affair with a slave. The last book was among Jackie's greatest publishing successes, having sold more than 2 million copies.

At a press briefing for *In the Russian Style*'s publication, a reporter asked her how her children had viewed the book.

"Rapidly," she said.

The word also summed up how her career went at Viking.

In 1977, Guinzburg got a call from literary agent Deborah Owen.

"I've got this manuscript," she said. "And I know what you're going to think of it but I still need a fast response from you."

The novel was called *Shall We Tell the President*, by the British writer Jeffrey Archer. The story involved Ted Kennedy as president in 1984, and an assassination plot against him. Guinzburg and Cork Smith had read the manuscript and thought it was OK. The author's reputation was well established; his last several books had been successful thrillers.

Guinzburg went to see Jackie about it.

"I have a manuscript and a problem," he told her.

"Is it good?"

"He's a good storyteller . . . but it's an assassination plot."

"Of who?"

"Ted Kennedy."

Jackie winced. "It doesn't succeed?" she pleaded.

"No."

"Will someone else publish it if we don't?"

"Yes."

"Do I have to work on it?"

"No—not at all."

She told Guinzburg that she appreciated that he had turned down other commercial books to protect her. And she was not going to stand in his way this time.

The trouble came when the *New York Times Book Review* panned the book and used a reflexive pronoun like a weapon directed at Jackie, saying: "Anybody associated with its publication should be ashamed of herself."

With that one final word in one of the most important publishing outlets, Jackie flew into a rage. And, as Guinzburg recalled, the whole Kennedy tribe came down on her, causing her to panic and cave. She was so used to being protected; she couldn't handle the implication that she had had something to do with the book, even if it was fiction, especially because the Kennedys were also upset about it. She cleaned out her desk and resigned through Nancy Tuckerman, who was pressed into action as her spokesman when necessary, even though she worked at Doubleday. Guinzburg was devastated. In the months before he died in 2010, he could still grow visibly sad when discussing why Jackie quit and said her leaving Viking remained one of his great regrets in life.

Not long after severing her relationship with Guinzburg and Viking, Jackie accepted another editing position—at Doubleday. There she edited about ninety books over the span of her career, including ones about Marie Antoinette, Louis XV, Napoleon, and Stalin. She also worked on books about American royalty: Princess Grace, John and Yoko, Fred Astaire, and Michael Jackson. Her interest in preservation continued through books such as *How to Save Your Own Street*, a collaboration with Urban Design Group of the Department of City Planning in New York, by Raquel Ramati; as well as *Stanford White's New York*, a biography of the leading Beaux-Arts architect by David Garrard Lowe. Jackie had first met the author in 1981 when they were both fighting to save another lovely building in New York, St. Bartholomew's Church on Park Avenue. Stanford White had been murdered in 1906 by an obsessed person who shot the architect three times during a performance at Madison Square Garden. At the author's book party, attended by one of White's grandsons, Jackie asked Lowe, "How did your father turn out?"[6] She clearly wondered about the effects an assassination could have on a surviving son.

In between, the books were eclectic: A Carly Simon children's series; an Egyptian trilogy by a Nobel Prize–winning author; literary fiction by up-and-comers, whose edits she would send back with the notes signed *"Bon Courage!"*[7]

She worked at Doubleday until she became quite ill, dying

at 1040 Fifth of non-Hodgkin's lymphoma on May 19, 1994. "My mother died surrounded by her friends and her family and her books, and the people and the things that she loved," John Jr. told the media camped outside her home. Maurice Tempelsman, the diamond merchant and financial adviser she first began seeing in 1975, did not divorce his wife. But he remained her loyal companion, arms linked as they strolled through Central Park, together for the holidays and for Jackie's transition into grandparenthood. He was there when she took her last breath.

On the day she was buried at Arlington National Cemetery—not just next to her first husband but among many other legendary men—the Municipal Art Society set out a memorial book made of parchment for mourners to sign inside Grand Central Terminal. Since that January morning in 1975 when she called the MAS office asking to get involved, Jackie had been the face of the fight to save the station, popping up publicly every time the issue was back in court. On July 12, 1976, anticipating Penn Central filing a brief to upset the Appellate Division's ruling, there was Jackie, participating in a stunt to light the station's facade for the first time, saying, "It's a beautiful building. And I think a city that's proud of itself should accent its beauty and make its people proud."[8] The following year, when the New York State Court of Appeals was about to begin hearing Penn Central's case, she participated in press conferences and a massive public lunchtime rally on the terminal's Park Avenue ramp with other celebrities, including Steve Allen (the first host of *The Tonight Show*) and

Alistair Cooke of *Masterpiece Theatre*. The court, once again, ruled against Penn, which decided to take the case to the US Supreme Court. In her final and most memorable public relations feat for Grand Central, Jackie rode the "Landmark Express," a train from New York to Washington, to drum up support for preservation.[9] The justices sided with Jackie and the Municipal Art Society, 6 to 3, saying they did not believe that "land-marking" Grand Central constituted a "taking" of the property requiring the city to pay Penn Central.[10] The decision affirmed that it was good for cities to protect their old buildings and it led to the creation of historic preservation laws across the country. The reverberations for this Supreme Court decision are still felt today; *Penn Central v. New York City* remains one of the most frequently cited cases in constitutional law.[11]

In the days after Jackie's death, a line of a thousand people waited inside Grand Central to sign the memorial book in front of a steel plaque that read, in part: JACQUELINE KENNEDY ONASSIS LED THE FIGHT TO SAVE THIS BEAUTIFUL TERMINAL. Janet Feldman of Manhattan was among them. She gripped a pen and wrote, "Dear John and Caroline, she taught us how to mourn; she taught us how to live; she taught us how to die. May her memory continue to inspire us all."[12]

ACKNOWLEDGMENTS

I am deeply grateful for the support of my family—especially my husband, Anthony Flint, and my parents, John and Gloria Cassidy—the glue that kept it all together. To my agent, Richard Abate; my editor, Claire Wachtel; and my researcher, Anne Baker, thank you for your dedication at every step of the way. Many people interviewed for this book were generous with their time, and their recollections helped this story come alive; I truly appreciate your contributions. And finally, the archives and helpful staff at the Municipal Art Society and the John F. Kennedy Library were invaluable resources. I thank you all.

NOTES

Prologue

1. http://data.bls.gov/PDQ/servlet/SurveyOutputServlet.

Chapter One: The Wife

1. Evans, 7–11.

2. Kennedy, Jacqueline, 219–20.

3. "Aristotle Onassis Dies of Pneumonia at American Hospital in Paris," *New York Times*, March 16, 1975.

4. Bradford, 344.

5. Evans, 38.

6. Evans, 39.

7. AP, "Jackie on Way to Greece Today," *Boston Herald*, Oct. 1, 1963.

8. Aristotle Onassis's FBI file, Bufile:100-125834, obtained under the Freedom of Information Act.

9. UPI, "Hodges Raps Roosevelt Cruise Critics," *Washington Post*, Oct. 23, 1963; Julius Dascha, "Inquiry Told Agriculture Dept. Withheld Data on Onassis Pact," *Washington Post-Times Herald*, Oct. 29, 1963; Drew Pearson, "First Lady's Cruise Causes Stir," *Washington Post-Times Herald*; Oct. 17, 1963.

10. UPI, "Turks Cheers Jacqueline," *Boston Globe*, Oct. 7, 1963; AP, "Jacqueline, Guests Isle-Hop in Aegean," *Boston Globe*, Oct. 9, 1963; UPI, "Jacqueline Takes a Fall at Delphi," *Boston Globe*, Oct. 13, 1963; UPI, "Jacqueline Meets Moroccan Monarch," *Boston Globe*, Oct. 14, 1963.

11. UPI, "Onassis Calls at White House," *Washington Post and Times Herald*, Nov. 28, 1963.

12. Nicholas von Hoffman, "A Life Lived in the Interest of Luxury and Rapacity," *Washington Post*, March 21, 1975.

13. Moutsatsos, 153–59.

14. Heymann, *A Woman Named Jackie*, 488–93; Anderson, 190–92.

15. Bradford, 341, 353.

16. Moutsatsos, 61.

17. Keogh, 9.

18. Adler, 196.

19. Ibid.

20. Caroline Kennedy talk at the JFK Library, Oct. 3, 2011.

21. Flora Lewis, "At His Table at Maxim's, He Reminisced," *New York Times*, March 16, 1975.

22. Maxine Cheshire, "A Last Summer on the *Christina?*" *Washington Post*, June 29, 1975.

23. Noel Hudson, "Church on Skorpios Readied," *Boston Globe*, Oct. 19, 1968.

24. Cafarakis, 71.

25. AP, "Reward Offered in Death of Onassis' Son," *Milwaukee Journal*, Dec. 24, 1974.

26. AP, "Onassis Will Give Up His Airline to Greece," *New York Daily News*, Jan. 16, 1975.

27. AP, "Onassis Will Give Up His Airline to Greece," *New York Daily News*; "Onassis, Bargaining from Weakness," *Economist*, Feb. 1, 1975, 78.

28. John Corry, "Onassis Said to Have Planned Divorce, Provided $3-Million for Widow in Will," *New York Times*, April 12, 1975.

29. Jack Anderson and Les Whitten, "Columns on Mrs. Onassis Denounced," *Washington Post*, May 9, 1975; Anderson, 287.

30. Evans, 287.

31. People column, *Time*, Jan. 13, 1975.

32. Suzy Says column, *New York Daily News*, Jan. 5, 1975.

33. AP, "Kennedy Chair Sells for $300," *Los Angeles Times*.

34. People, *Time*, Jan. 20, 1975.

35. Fern Eckman and Helen Dudar, "A Routine Auction, Until Jackie's 'Stuff' Arrived," *New York Post*, Jan. 8, 1975.

Chapter Two: The Writer

1. Florence Fabricant, "La Caravelle, a French Legend, Is Closing after 43 Years," *New York Times*, May 12, 2004.

2. Meehan, 112.

3. Talk of the Town, *The New Yorker*, May 30, 1994.

4. Thayer, 7; Radziwill, 134.

5. Birmingham as reprinted in the *Boston Herald*, Oct. 29, 1978.

6. Thayer, 45.

7. *Time*, Jan. 20, 1961.

8. Thayer, 20.

9. Thayer, 20.

10. Thayer, 20.

11. Thayer, 55.

12. Thayer, 21.

13. Thayer, 31.

14. Thayer, 39.

15. Thayer, 34.

16. Radziwill, 135.

17. "Jacqueline Kennedy in the White House," Arthur M. Schlesinger, *Jacqueline Kennedy: The White House Years* (Boston: Little, Brown and Co., 2001), 7.

18. Thayer, 63–64.

19. *Time*, Jan. 20, 1961.

20. Schlesinger, 17.

21. Friedan, 58.

22. Thayer, 77.

23. Thayer, 76.

24. Thayer, 60.

25. Roberta Mackey, "Woman with Everything," *Boston Traveler*, Oct. 10, 1960.

26. Thayer, 82.

27. JBKO, *Vogue* material, box 1, "Prizewinner," *Vogue*, Aug. 1994, JFK Library.

28. JBKO, *Vogue* material, box 1, Fashion—Question 2, JFK Library.

29. JBKO, *Vogue* material, box 1, Feature—Question 4, JFK Library.

30. JBKO, *Vogue* material, box 1, Feature—Question 3, JFK Library.

31. *Bouvier*, unpaginated.

32. *Bouvier*, unpaginated.

33. Thayer, 83.

34. Ballard, 2.

35. Bradford, 49.

36. JBKO, *Vogue* Material, box 1, JFK Library, Letter to Miss Campbell, May 27, 1951.

37. Dorothy McCardle, Jacqueline Kennedy Series, no. 2, *Washington Post and Times-Herald*, Sept. 29, 1960.

38. Bradford, 5.

39. Bradford, 52.

40. Thayer, 84.

41. Chuck Conconi, "Girl Reporter," *Washingtonian*, July 1994, 40. Same citation for the entire scene.

42. Chuck Conconi, "Girl Reporter," *Washingtonian*, July 1994, 40.

43. Thayer, 84.

44. Thayer, 84.

45. Dorothy McCardle, Jacqueline Kennedy Series, no. 3, *Washington Post and Times-Herald*, Sept. 30, 1960.

46. Chuck Conconi, "Girl Reporter," *Washingtonian*, July 1994, 40.

47. "Jackie: Behind the Myth," PBS Home Video, DVD, Suzanne Bauman, director, 1999.

48. Bradford, 57.

49. Heymann, *A Woman Named Jackie*, 108.

50. Heymann, *A Woman Named Jackie*, 108.

51. Charles L. Bartlett Oral History Interview, JFK Library, JFK #1, 1/6/1965, 20; Bradford, 56.

52. Charles L. Bartlett Oral History, Interview, JFK Library, JFK #1, 1/6/1965, 21-22.

53. *Washington Times-Herald*, Nov. 7, 1952.

54. Jacqueline Bouvier, "Picnic Lunches Help Crowd Wait for Inaugural Parade," *Washington Times-Herald*, Jan. 21, 1953.

55. Mary R. Thayer, "Jacqueline Kennedy," *Ladies Home Journal*, Feb. 27, 1961.

56. Chuck Conconi, "Girl Reporter," *Washingtonian*, July 1994, 43.

57. Chuck Conconi, "Girl Reporter," *Washingtonian*, July 1994, 42.

58. John Harris, "Kennedy Fiancée Sketched and Wrote about the Coronation," *Boston Globe*, June 26, 1953.

59. Janet Lee Bouvier Auchincloss Oral History Interview, JFK Library, JFK #1, 9/5/1964, 2.

60. Thayer, 92.

61. Spoto, 80–96.

62. Thayer, 97.

63. Janet Lee Bouvier Auchincloss Oral History, by Joan Braden, JFK Library, 9/5/1964, 6.

64. Parmet, 103–7.

65. Clayton Fitchey, "Jacqueline's View of JFK," *Boston Globe*, Nov. 22, 1966.

66. Parmet, 313–14.

67. Sorensen, 146.

68. JFK Personal Papers, *Profiles in Courage*, boxes 27–35, JFK Library.

69. Interview with Theodore Sorensen, Aug. 11, 2010.

70. Jacqueline Kennedy: Historic Conversations, oral history with Arthur M. Schlesinger Jr., 1964, xii.

71. Interview with Theodore Sorensen; Schlesinger, 321.

72. Mrs. John F. Kennedy, "Campaign Wife," Sept. 16, 1960, released by the DNC, ready reference no. 36, JFK Library.

73. Mrs. John F. Kennedy, "Campaign Wife," Nov. 1, 1960, released by the DNC, ready reference no. 36, JFK Library.

74. www.newyorker.com/magazine/timeline.

75. Talk of the Town, *The New Yorker*, May 30, 1994, 34.

76. Notes on People, *New York Times*, Jan. 4, 1975.

77. Talk of the Town, *The New Yorker*, Jan. 13, 1975, 27–28.

78. People, *Time*, Jan. 20, 1975.

79. Newsmakers, *Newsweek*, Jan. 20, 1975, 47.

80. Dorothy McCardle, "A Few Words from the 'Anonymous' Jacqueline Onassis," *Washington Post*, Jan. 8, 1975, B1.

Chapter Three: The Preservationist

1. Interviews and correspondence with Laurie Beckelman, beginning Jan. 2010.

2. Interviews and correspondence with Kent Barwick, beginning Jan. 2010.

3. Belle and Leighton, 75.

4. Gilmartin, 403.

5. Jean Sprain Wilson, AP, "She Will Never Again Be the Same Woman," *Boston Globe*, Nov. 14, 1965.

6. Interview with Paul Goldberger, April 16, 2010.

7. Klein, 96–98.

8. Bradford, 7.

9. "The First Lady: She Tells Her Plans for the White House," *Life*, Sept. 1, 1961, 62.

10. "The First Lady: She Tells Her Plans for the White House," *Life*, Sept. 1, 1961, 62.

11. Kennedy, Jacqueline, 131–32.

12. Transcription of a conversation with Mrs. Henry Parish, II, Parish-Hadley Associates Inc. Records, JFK Library, box #2, 1–3.

13. Transcription of a conversation with Mrs. Henry Parish, II, Parish-Hadley Associates Inc.Records, JFK Library, box #2, 1.

14. Kennedy, Jacqueline, 131.

15. Kennedy, Jacqueline, 132.

16. West, 192.

17. West, 192.

18. AP, "Visits White House after Leaving Hospital," *Boston Globe*, Dec. 9, 1960.

19. Jacqueline Kennedy: Historic Conversations, oral history with Arthur M. Schlesinger Jr., 1964, 132.

20. Hugh Sidey, "Election 2000: This Old House," *Time*, Nov. 20, 2000.

21. Bradford ,143.

22. West, 193.

23. Kennedy, Jacqueline, 132.

24. J. Bernard West Oral History Interview, JFK Library, JFK #1, 1967, 2–4.

25. Leamer, 515.

26. Leamer, 515.

27. DAZ and Richard Harkness, "A New First Lady, A New Mood: Mrs. Kennedy Is Bringing Changes to Her New Home—Just Like Many of Her Predecessors," *New York Times*, April 23, 1961.

28. Joseph Karitas Oral History Interview, JFK Library, JFK #1, 6/23/1964, 12–13.

29. Janet Lee Bouvier Auchincloss Oral History, JFK Library, 9/5/1964, 12.

30. "Jacqueline Kennedy in the White House," Arthur M. Schlesinger, *Jacqueline Kennedy: The White House Years* (Boston: Little, Brown and Co., 2001), 7.

31. Isabelle Shelton, "Jackie Gets Fair Shake in Book on JFK," *Boston Globe*, April 13, 1971.

32. Jacqueline Kennedy: Historic Conversations, oral history with Arthur M. Schlesinger Jr., 1964, 43.

33. "Jacqueline Kennedy in the White House," Arthur M. Schlesinger, *Jacqueline Kennedy: The White House Years* (Boston: Little, Brown and Co., 2001), 6.

34. Parish-Hadley Associates Inc. Records, JFK Library, box 1, signed Philip J. Jerome.

35. J. Bernard West Oral History Interview, JFK Library, JFK #1, 1967, 5, 6, 11.

36. Abbot and Rice, 10.

37. Bowles et al., 6.

38. DAZ and Richard Harkness, "A New First Lady, A New Mood: Mrs. Kennedy Is Bringing Changes to Her New Home—Just Like Many of Her Predecessors," *New York Times*, April 23, 1961.

39. www.udel.edu/PR/Messenger/94/4/35.html.

40. Parish-Hadley Associates Inc. Records, JFK Library, box 1.

41. Abbott and Rice, 206.

42. Talk of the Town, "Remembering Jackie," *The New Yorker*, May 30, 1994.

43. Bernard L. Boutin Oral History Interview, JFK Library, JFK #1, 6/3/1964.

44. Parish-Hadley Associates Inc, box 1, JFK Library.

45. Lawrence J. Arata Oral History Interview, JFK Library, JFK #1, 1964.

46. Parish-Hadley Associates Inc., JFK Library, box #1, Loeb Letter, July 7, 1961.

47. Parish-Hadley Associates Inc., JFK Library, box #1, Mr. John Loeb, Oval Room, White House.

48. White House Social Files, JFK Library, box 947 (White House Library only).

49. White House Social Files, JFK Library, box 947 (White House Library only); memo from Letitia Baldrige to Jackie, Jan. 30, 1962; memo from Baldrige to Mr. Rice, July 10, 1962.

50. AP, "For the White House First Lady Seeking Old Books," *Washington Post and Times-Herald*, May 27, 1962.

51. *The White House: An Historic Guide*, 150.

52. "The First Lady: She Tells Her Plans for the White House," *Life*, Sept. 1, 1961, 63.

53. Roberta Mackey, "Jackie Loves Georgetown Home," *Boston Traveler*, Oct. 14, 1960.

54. Benjamin C. Bradlee, "The Jackie Kennedy Show," *Washington Post*, May 19, 1975.

55. Benjamin C. Bradlee, "The Jackie Kennedy Show," *Washington Post*, May 19, 1975.

56. Bowles et al., 71.

57. Kennedy, Jacqueline, 137.

58. Elizabeth Sullivan, "White House Tour with Mrs. John F. Kennedy," *Boston Sunday Globe*, Feb. 11, 1962.

59. Tape of White House tour, http://toobworld.blogspot.com/2010/02/toobworld-meets-real-world-2141962.html.

60. Richard Moe and Leonard A. Zax, "Jackie's Washington: How She Rescued the City's History," *Washington Post*, May 29, 1994.

61. "Capital Plagued by Old Buildings," *New York Times*, March 10, 1957.

62. William Walton Oral History Interview, JFK Library, JFK #1, 3/30/1993, 39.

63. Marjorie Hunter, "Historic Square in Washington Will Be Demolished," *New York Times*, Feb. 14, 1962.

64. www.preservationnation.org/forum/resource-center/forum-library/public-articles/the-historic-preservation-legacy-of.html.

65. Richard Moe and Leonard A. Zax, "Jackie's Washington: How She Rescued the City's History," *Washington Post*, May 29, 1994; Sarah Booth Conroy, "Preserving Lafayette Square," *Washington Post, Home Magazine*, May 26, 1994, 17.

66. Bradford, 237.

67. Marjorie Hunter, "President Hails Historic Square: Says New Lafayette Design Should Be Urban Example," *New York Times*, Oct. 18, 1962.

68. Letter from JBKO to Bill Walton, June 8, 1962, Walton Papers, box 1, letters from Kennedys, JFK Library.

69. Marjorie Hunter, "President Hails Historic Square: Says New Lafayette Design Should Be Urban Example," *New York Times*, Oct. 18, 1962.

70. Marjorie Hunter, "Girlhood Home of Mrs. Kennedy Optional for Luxury Apartments," *New York Times*, Jan. 14, 1962.

71. Dorothy McCardle, "Twice-Used JFK Home Opening to Visitors," *Boston Globe*, July 24, 1968; Dorothy McCardle, "Jacqueline Sketched Own Plan for New Mountaintop Retreat," *Boston Globe*, Dec. 11, 1962.

72. Everard Munsey, "McLean Residents Try to Halt Merrywood Sale," *Washington Post and Times-Herald*, April 25, 1962.

73. Everard Munsey, "Special Fairfax Grand Jury to Probe Merrywood Rezoning," *Washington Post andTimes-Herald*, April 28, 1962.

74. Walter B. Douglas, "Suit Won't Halt Sale of Merrywood," *Washington Post and Times-Herald*, May 29, 1962.

75. Everard Munsey, "Auchincloss Cites Sales Contract, Stands Firm in McLean Rezoning," *Washington Post and Times-Herald*, April 26, 1962.

76. William Chapman, "The Merrywood Flap," *Washington Post and Times-Herald*, Jan. 4, 1964.

77. "Interior Dept. Sues to Block Merrywood Project," *Washington Post and Times-Herald*, Nov. 16, 1963, A1.

78. "Interior Dept. Posts Signs Blocking Merrywood Work," *Washington Post and Times-Herald*, Nov. 17, 1963, B1.

79. "Builder Saves Hillside Where Jackie Played," *Boston Globe*, Oct. 19, 1965; Hank Burchard, "Jackie's Girlhood Home to Be Posh Development," *Boston Globe*, Dec. 26, 1967; Maxine Cheshire, "The Dickersons of Merrywood," *Washington Post and Times-Herald*, Aug. 17, 1969.

80. Joseph Karitas Oral History Interview, JFK Library, JFK #1, 6/23/1964, 22–23.

81. Emma Brown, "John Carl Warnecke Dies at 91," *Washington Post*, April 23, 2010.

82. "Percy E. Sutton, Political Trailblazer, Dies at 89," *New York Times*, Dec. 27, 2009.

83. "Jackie: Behind the Myth," PBS Home Video, DVD, Suzanne Bauman, director, 1999.

84. Interview with Ed Koch, Jan. 27, 2010.

85. Interview with Hugh Hardy, March 1, 2010.

86. "Court Rules Against Landmark: Grand Central Case Decided," *Preservation News* 15 (March 1975): 3.

87. George Arzt and Steven Marcus, "Beame Firing 4050 More," *New York Post*, Jan. 15, 1975.

88. Diane Henry, "Jackie Onassis Fights for Cause," *New York Times*, Jan. 31, 1975; letter from Robert F. Wagner to Grand Central Committee Members, Jan. 29, 1975, courtesy MAS; letter from Robert F. Wagner to Mayor Beame, Jan. 29, 1975, courtesy MAS.

89. "Jackie: Behind the Myth," PBS Home Video, DVD, Suzanne Bauman, director, 1999.

90. Eleanor Swertlow, "Jackie Onassis Enters Battle for Rescue of Grand Central," *New York Daily News*, Jan. 31, 1975.

91. Klein, 276.

92. Gilmartin, 405.

93. Stein and Plimpton, 27.

94. Interviews with Hugh Hardy, March 1, 2010; Fred Papert, Jan. 27, 2010; Margot Wellington, Dec. 4, 2009.

95. "Jacqueline's Letter Sold for $3000," *Boston Globe*, March 20, 1964.

96. Press release dated March 3, 1975, MAS archives.

Chapter Four: The Widow

1. UPI, "Onassis Has Flu, Brother-in-Law Says, *Los Angeles Times*, Feb. 5, 1975.

2. AP, "Onassis' Condition Blamed on Very Heavy Influenza," *Los Angeles Times*, Feb. 8, 1975.

3. Liz Smith, "Alone Again: Aristotle Onassis's Death Has Left Jacqueline Kennedy Onassis Twice Widowed in 12 Years," *People*, March 31, 1975.

4. "Greece: The Ailing King," *Time*, Feb. 17, 1975.

5. AP, "Onassis in Paris for Treatment, Wife with Him," *Los Angeles Times*, Feb. 7, 1975.

6. www.hellomagazine.com/celebrities/2006/07/20/athinaonassis/.

7. Photo caption, *London Times*, Feb. 5, 1975.

8. Klein, 277.

9. Anderson, 289.

10. Evans, 288–90.

11. Moutsatsos, 294.

12. AP, "Onassis' Condition Blamed on Very Heavy Influenza," *Los Angeles Times*, Feb. 8, 1975.

13. "Onassis Operation," *London Times*, Feb. 11, 1975; Klein, 280.

14. "Operation on Mr. Onassis Is Successful," *London Times*, Feb. 20, 1975.

15. UPI, "Onassis Has Jaundice; Prognosis Still Guarded," *Los Angeles Times*, Feb. 13, 1975.

16. Guthrie, 173; Klein, 280.

17. Anderson, 289.

18. Notes on People, *New York Times*, Feb. 20, 1975.

19. www.knoxnews.com/news/2010/mar/27/former-nun-from-new-york-helped
-appalachian/.

20. "A New Life for Jackie," *Boston Sunday Globe*, Nov. 22, 1964.

21. Raleigh Allsbrook, AP, "A $200,000 Apartment," *Boston Globe*, July 30, 1964.

22. Anderson, 104, 127–28.

23. Linda Bird Francke, "Legacy of the Golden Greek," *Newsweek*, March 31, 1975, 82;
Klein, 281.

24. Wire services, "Aristotle Onassis, 69, Dies; Parlayed $60 into Millions," *Los Angeles Times*, March 16, 1975.

25. Lawrence, 8.

26. Interview with Ron Galella, Feb. 8, 2010.

27. "Mrs. Onassis Flies from Here to Paris," *New York Times*, March 16, 1975.

28. Bowles et al., 121.

29. Bowles et al., 126.

30. AP, "Mrs. Onassis' Inheritance Reportedly $120 Million," *Los Angeles Times*, March 17, 1975.

31. Flora Lewis, "Mrs. Onassis Visits Bier; Family Arranging Funeral," *New York Times*, March 17, 1975.

32. "Onassis' Intimates Gathering," *Washington Post*, March 18, 1975.

33. Schlesinger, 1026.

34. Lawrence J. Arata Oral History Interview, JFK Library, JFK #1, 6/23/1964.

35. Stein and Plimpton, 127.

36. Moutsatsos, 298.

37. AP, "Widow Kisses Coffin: Onassis Buried in Cypress Grove," *Los Angeles Times*, March 19, 1975.

38. Moutsatsos, 299.

39. Moutsatsos, 283, 298.

40. "What Now for Jackie Onassis?" *Time*, March 31, 1975.

41. AP, "Widow Kisses Coffin: Onassis Buried in Cypress Grove," *Los Angeles Times*, March 19, 1975.

42. Evans, 240–44.

43. AP, "Widow Kisses Coffin: Onassis Buried in Cypress Grove," *Los Angeles Times*, March 19, 1975.

44. "Onassis Buried on Hillside in Skorpios," *New York Times*, March 19, 1975.

45. AP, "Aristotle 'Rescued Me'—Mrs. Onassis," *Los Angeles Times*, May 17, 1975; Moutsatsos, 302.

Chapter Five: The Target

1. "Rally Held for Grand Central to Become a Landmark Again," *New York Times*, April 16, 1975.

2. AP, "Mother Calls Talk of Onassis Divorce False," *Los Angeles Times*, April 19, 1975.

3. Jack Anderson and Les Whitten, "Mrs. Onassis Sells Used Wardrobe," *Washington Post*, April 16, 1975.

4. AP, "Mother Calls Talk of Onassis Divorce False," *Los Angeles Times*, April 19, 1975.

5. Moutsatsos, 349.

6. People, *Time*, May 5, 1975.

7. Moutsatsos, 349.

8. *London Times*, April 20, 1975.

9. Moutsatsos, 153–56.

10. Moutsatsos, 158.

11. Moutsatsos, 350–52.

12. AP, "Aristotle 'Rescued Me'—Mrs. Onassis," *Los Angeles Times*, May 17, 1975.

13. Jack Anderson and Les Whitten, "Columns of Mrs. Onassis Denounced," *Washington Post*, May 9, 1975.

14. Benjamin C. Bradlee, "A TV Interview, Rehashing a Party, the Children," *Washington Post*, May 22, 1975.

15. Sally Quinn, "Pomp, Circumstance and the Secret Service," *Washington Post*, June 6, 1975.

16. "Onassis Will Gives Widow Allowance," *Washington Post*, June 8, 1975.

17. AP, "Onassis Wrote Will to Daughter," *Los Angeles Times*, June 8, 1975; "Onassis Will Gives Widow Allowance," *Washington Post*, June 8, 1975.

Chapter Six: The Seeker

1. www.sulgraveclub.org/default.aspx?p=GenericModuleDefault&NoModResize=1 &NoNav=1&ShowFooter=False&ModID=56273&modtype=Clubnbsp;History &sl=1&vnf=0&ssid=0&dpageid=202759.

2. Kennedy, Jacqueline, 170.

3. Kennedy, Jacqueline, 349.

4. Interview with Letitia Baldrige, March 6, 2010.

5. Schiff, 294–95.

6. Interview with Letitia Baldrige, March 6, 2010.

7. Kate Lang, "You Can Always Tell a Place," *Boston Globe*, April 24, 1961.

8. Clayton Freitchey, "Jacqueline's View of JFK," *Boston Globe*, Nov. 22, 1966; Schlesinger, 105.

9. Dorothy McCardle, "Jackie Covers Ike's Inaugural," *Washington Post*, Sept. 29, 1960.

10. www.udel.edu/PR/Messenger/94/4/35.html; *Washington Post, Home Magazine*, "Legacy of Style," May 26, 1994, 18.

11. AP, "Widow's Memoir: 'I Don't Think There Is Any Consolation,' " *Boston Globe*, May 22, 1994.

12. JBKO Oral History, Jan. 11, 1974, LBJ Library; Anderson, 136; Klein, 93–94.

13. "The Presidency: Battle of the Book," *Time*, Dec. 23, 1966.

14. "The Presidency: Battle of the Book," *Time*, Dec. 23, 1966.

15. Sam Kashner, "A Clash of Camelots," *Vanity Fair*, Oct. 2009, 242–58; AP, "Harper & Row, Kennedy Lawyers Negotiating More Book Deletions," *Boston Globe*, Dec. 23, 1966; AP, "JFK Book Battle," *Boston Globe*, Dec. 18, 1966; AP, "Mrs. JFK Sues to Block Book," *Boston Globe*, Dec. 16, 1966; AP, "References to LBJ Disturb Jacqueline," *Boston Globe*, Dec. 15, 1966; Liz Smith, "Jackie Comes off Her Pedestal," *Boston Globe*, Jan. 11, 1967; William Manchester, "The Day JFK Died," *Look*, Feb. 7, 1967, 41–56.

16. Sam Kashner, "A Clash of Camelots," *Vanity Fair*, Oct. 2009, 258.

17. Interview with Jason Epstein, Jan. 27, 2010; Epstein, 127–30.

18. Interview with Thomas Guinzburg, June 10, 2010.

19. JFK Library journal exhibit.

20. www.theparisreview.org/letters-essays/6069/thomas-guinzburg-peter-matthiessen.

21. "Curator Expediting Temple's Shipment," *New York Times*, Oct. 16, 1967.

22. Malcolm Carter, "An Ancient Temple Rises at the Met," *New York Times*, July 6, 1975; Notes on People, *New York Times*, June 12, 1975; Lawrence, 173.

Chapter Seven: The Hot Prospect

1. Maxine Cheshire, "A Role in Tycoon for Mrs. Onassis?" *Washington Post*, July 13, 1975.

2. Notes on People, *New York Times*, June 26, 1975.

3. New York Intelligence column, *New York*, "Jackie and Nancy: Partying?" July 21, 1975.

4. Maxine Cheshire, "Memoirs of Jackie Onassis?" *Washington Post*, July 3, 1975.

5. Bradford, 372.

6. Reuters, "Miss Onassis Weds Son of Greek Shipping Magnate," *London Times*, July 23, 1975.

7. Davis, 216–17.

8. "People: The Multimillion-Dollar Match," *Time*, Aug. 4, 1975.

9. Newsmakers, *Newsweek*, Aug. 4, 1975, 48.

10. Staff and wire services, "Christina Onassis Dies; Investigation Ordered," *Los Angeles Times*, Nov. 20, 1988; Michelle Green, "Fate's Captive: Dead at 37, Christina Onassis Leaves an Empire and Burdens She Could Never Escape to Her Daughter, Athina," *People*, Dec. 5, 1988.

11. "Traces of Sedatives Present in Christina's Body," *New Straights Times*, Reuter, Dec. 12, 1988.

12. Jack Anderson with Les Whitten, "Jackie-Ari Relationship Not Happy," *Washington Post*, April 17, 1975.

13. Peter Beard, personal correspondence, July 1, 2010.

14. Robert D. McFadden, "Death of First Lady: The Companion; Quietly at Her Side, Public at the End," *New York Times*, May 24, 1994.

15. Telegram 641 from the embassy in Zaire to the Department of State, Jan. 23, 1975, 1000Z.

Chapter Eight: The Working Woman

1. Interviews and correspondence with Rebecca Singleton, Sept. 20, Dec. 1, Dec. 6, and Dec. 14, 2010.

2. Elizabeth Peer, "Jackie on Her Own," *Newsweek*, Sept. 29, 1975.

3. Gloria Steinem, "Why Does This Woman Work," *Ms.*, March 1979.

4. Singleton correspondence, Nov. 19, 2011.

5. AP, "Going to Dinner," *Los Angeles Times*, Sept. 18, 1975.

6. Interview with Barbara Burn, Dec. 11, 2010.

7. Interview with Barbara Burn, Dec. 11, 2010.

8. John A. Conaway, "Jackie's Mail," *Newsweek*, Oct. 20, 1975, 17.

9. Interview with Barbara Burn, Dec. 11, 2010.

10. Elizabeth Peer, "Jackie on Her Own," *Newsweek*, Sept. 29, 1975, 80.

11. "Her Friends Remember Jacqueline Kennedy Onassis," *New York*, May 30, 1994, 27.

12. Vivian Cadden and Helene Markel, "The Surprising New Life of Jacqueline Onassis," *McCall's*, Feb. 1976, 180.

13. "Jackie's Little List," *New York*, Nov. 25, 1975.

14. Interviews with Conover Hunt and Miriam Schneir, June 19, 2010.

15. Anderson, 301–10.

Chapter Nine: The Empty Nester

1. Suzy Says, *New York Daily News*, Jan. 15, 1975, 12.

2. People, *New York Times*, Sept. 3, 1975.

3. Robert Parker, "MP and Kennedy Daughter Escape London Death Bomb," *London Times*, Oct. 24, 1975; Bernard Weinraub, "Bomb Kills a Doctor Near London Home of Caroline Kennedy," *New York Times*, Oct. 24, 1975.

4. "Caroline Kennedy Back in Class after Bomb Explosion," *Chicago Daily News* item in the *Boston Globe*, Oct. 24, 1975; *Boston Globe*, Nov. 2, 1975.

5. Peter Benson, "Caroline Kennedy—On Her Own in London . . . and Loving It!" *Good Housekeeping*, April, 1976, 215–16.

6. Nadine Brozan, "Tie Is Tied to a Cause," *New York Times*, Oct. 4, 1975.

7. Sally Quinn, "Projecting a New Image or Not, Jacqueline Onassis Is an Event." *Washington Post*, Nov. 14, 1975.

8. "La Côte Basque 1965," Truman Capote, *Esquire*, Nov. 1975, 112.

9. "La Côte Basque 1965," Truman Capote, *Esquire*, Nov. 1975, 113.

10. "La Côte Basque 1965," Truman Capote, *Esquire*, Nov. 1975, 118.

11. Charlotte Curtis, "Lee Radziwill in Search of Herself," *McCall's* 1975, 32–40; Judy Klemesrud, "For Lee Radziwill, Budding Careers and New Life in New York," *New York Times*, Sept. 1, 1974.

12. "Jackie in Tehran," *Boston Globe*, July 1, 1972.

13. Sally Quinn, "A New Image or Not, Jacqueline Onassis Is an Event," *Washington Post*, Nov. 14, 1975.

14. Jackie Kroll, "The World on Film," *Newsweek*, Oct. 13, 1975, 103.

15. Notes on People, *New York Times*, April 24, 1973 and Sept. 21, 1972.

16. Bill Roder, Newsmakers column, *Newsweek*, Dec. 1, 1975, 60.

17. "New Doubts about Kennedy Killing," *London Times*, Nov. 19, 1975.

18. Laurence Stern, "JFK Friendship Related," *Washington Post*, Dec. 18, 1975.

19. Bradford, 382.

Epilogue

1. Kennedy, Jacqueline, 2.

2. "Portrait of a Presidential Wife," *Boston Globe*, Aug. 30, 1960.

3. Kennedy, Jacqueline, xxv.

4. Kennedy, Jacqueline, 202.

5. Dorothy Fleeson, "Her Greatest Innovation in the White House—Bouquets: Lunch with the President's Wife," April 13, 1961.

6. Lawrence, 240.

7. Darcey Steinke papers, special collections, Goucher College, Baltimore, MD.

8. Photo caption, *New York Times*, July 13, 1976.

9. Municipal Art Society, press releases.

10. *Penn Central Transportation Co. et al. v. New York City et al.*, 438 US 104 (1978).

11. Interview with Harvard professor Jerold S. Kayden.

12. Ray Sanchez, "Images of Jackie: Mourners Jam Grand Central Memorial," *New York Newsday*, May 25, 1994.

BIBLIOGRAPHY

Abbott, James A., and Elaine M. Rice. *Designing Camelot: The Kennedy White House Restoration.* New York: VNR, 1998.

Adler, Bill. *The Eloquent Jacqueline Kennedy Onassis.* New York: William Morrow, 2004.

Anderson, Christopher. *Jackie After Jack: A Portrait of the Lady.* New York: Warner Books, 1999.

Belle, John, and Maxine R. Leighton. *Grand Central: Gateway to a Million Lives.* New York: Norton, 2000.

Birmingham, Stephen. *Jacqueline Bouvier Kennedy Onassis.* New York: Grosset & Dunlap, 1978.

Bowles, Hamish, Arthur Schlesinger, and Rachel Lambert Mellon. *Jacqueline Kennedy: The White House Years.* Boston: Little, Brown, 2001.

Bradford, Sarah. *America's Queen: The Life of Jacqueline Kennedy Onassis.* New York: Penguin Books, 2000.

Bouvier, Jacqueline and Lee. *One Special Summer.* New York: Delacorte Press, 1974.

Cafarakis, Christian. *The Fabulous Onassis: His Life and Loves.* New York: Morrow, 1972.

Cheshire, Maxine. *Maxine Cheshire: Reporter.* Boston: Houghton Mifflin, 1978.

David, Lest. *Jacqueline Kennedy Onassis: The Woman She Has Become.* Secaucus: Carol Publishing Group, 1994.

Davis, L. J. *Onassis: Aristotle and Christina*. New York: St. Martin's Press, 1986.

DePauw, Linda Grant. *Remember the Ladies*. New York: Viking Press, 1976.

Dickerson, Nancy. *Among Those Present: A Reporter's View of Twenty-five Years in Washington*. New York: Random House, 1976.

Douglas, Susan J. *Where the Girls Are: Growing Up Female with the Mass Media*. New York: Times Books, Random House, 1994.

DuBois, Diana. *In Her Sister's Shadow: An Intimate Biography of Lee Radziwill*. Boston: Little, Brown and Co., 1995.

Epstein, Jason. *Eating: A Memoir*. New York: Random House, 2009.

Evans, Peter. *Nemesis*. New York: ReganBooks, 2004.

Friedan, Betty. *The Feminine Mystique*. New York: W. W. Norton, 2001 ed.

Gallagher, Mary Barelli. *My Life with Jacqueline Kennedy*. New York: David McKay Co., 1969.

Gilmartin, Gregory F. *Shaping the City: New York and the Municipal Art Society*. New York: Clarkson Potter, 1995.

Gross, Michael. *740 Park: The Story of the World's Richest Apartment Building*. New York: Broadway, 2005.

Guthrie, Lee. *Jackie: The Price of the Pedestal*. New York: Drake, 1978.

Hacket, Pat, ed. *The Andy Warhol Diaries*. New York: Warner Books, 1989.

Hamilton, Edith. *The Greek Way*. New York: Norton, 1971 ed.

Heymann, C. David. *A Woman Named Jackie: An Intimate Biography of Jacqueline Bouvier Kennedy Onassis*. New York: Pan, 1999.

Heymann, C. David. *Bobby and Jackie: A Love Story*. New York: Atria, 2009.

Kennedy, Jacqueline. *Historic Conversations on Life with John F. Kennedy*. New York: Hyperion, 2011.

Kennedy, John F. *Profiles in Courage*. New York: Harper & Bros., 1955.

Kennedy, Rose Fitzgerald. *Times to Remember*. New York: Doubleday, 1995.

Keogh, Pamela Clarke. *Jackie Style*. New York: HarperCollins, 2001.

Klein, Edward. *Just Jackie: Her Private Years*. New York: Ballantine Books, 1998.

Kuhn, William. *Reading Jackie: Her Autobiography in Books*. New York: Nan Talese, Doubleday, 2010.

Lawrence, Greg. *Jackie as Editor*. New York: Thomas Dunne Books, St. Martin's Press, 2011.

Leamer, Laurence. *The Kennedy Women: The Saga of an American Family*. New York: Ballantine Books, 1996.

Leisenring, L. Morris. "Lament for Lafayette Square." *AIA Journal* 35, no. 2 (Feb. 1961): 25–32.

Meehan, William F. *Conversations with William F. Buckley Jr.* Jackson, MS: University Press of Mississippi, 2009.

Mehta, Ved. *Mr. Shawn's* New Yorker: *The Invisible Art of Editing.* Woodstock: Overlook Press, 1998.

Moutsatsos, Kiki Feroudi. *The Onassis Women: An Eyewitness Account.* New York: G. P. Putnam's Sons, 1998.

Onassis, Jacqueline, ed. *In the Russian Style.* New York: Viking Press, Penguin, 1976.

Parmet, Herbert S. *Jack: The Struggles of John F. Kennedy.* New York: Dial Press, 1980.

Radziwill, Lee. *Happy Times.* New York: Assouline Publishing, 2000.

Schiff, Dorothy. *Men, Money & Magic: The Story of Dorothy Schiff.* New York: Coward, McCann & Geoghegan, Inc., 1976.

Schlesinger, Arthur. *A Thousand Days.* Boston: Houghton Mifflin Co., 1965.

Sgubin, Marta. *Cooking for Madam: Recipes and Reminisces from the Home of Jacqueline Kennedy Onassis.* New York: Scribner, 1998.

Sorensen, Theodore. *Counselor: A Life at the Edge of History.* New York: Harper Perennial, 2009.

Spoto, Donald. *Jacqueline Bouvier Kennedy Onassis: A Life.* New York: St. Martin's Press, 2000.

Stein, Jean, and George Plimpton. *American Journey: The Times of Robert Kennedy.* New York: Harcourt Brace Jovanovich, 1970.

Steinem, Gloria. *Outrageous Acts and Everyday Rebellions.* New York: Holt, Rinehart and Winston, 1983.

Thayer, Mary Van Rensselaer. *Jacqueline Bouvier Kennedy.* New York: Doubleday, 1961.

The Warren Commission. *The Assassination of President Kennedy.* New York: McGraw Hill, 1964.

West, J. B. *Upstairs at the White House.* New York: Coward, McCann & Geoghegan, Inc., 1973

White, Theodore. *The Making of the President.* New York: Atheneum, 1969.

White House Historical Association. *The White House: An Historic* Guide, 22nd ed., 2003.

Tina Cassidy, an acclaimed author and journalist, spent most of her career as a reporter and editor at the *Boston Globe*, where she wrote about everything from business to politics to fashion. Her previous book was *Birth: The Surprising History of How We Are Born*. She is also a public relations executive and lives in Massachusetts with her husband and their three sons.